CHRISTOLOGY

THE STUDY OF CHRIST

Daniel L. Akin

Christology
The Study of Christ

Daniel L. Akin

Published by Rainer Publishing
www.rainerpublishig.com

ISBN 978-0692381540

CONTENTS

INTRODUCTION

Most certainly, the mystery of godliness is great: [Jesus] was manifested in the flesh, justified in the Spirit, seen by angels, preached among the Gentiles, believed on in the world, taken up in glory.

(1 Timothy 3:16)

Christology—the study of the person and work of Jesus Christ—is the central doctrine of Christianity. From Genesis to Revelation, Scripture paints an incomparable portrait of the Word who "became flesh and took up residence among us" (John 1:14). With false portraits and inaccurate caricatures so prevalent in the 21st century, it is imperative that we embrace the Bible's teaching about Jesus of Nazareth. What we believe about Jesus—who he is and what he did—will shape greatly the rest of our theology (what we believe about the Bible, God, humanity, salvation, the Church and eschatology).

Answering the "Jesus Question" has provoked spirited debate throughout the history of the Church. In our postmodern, pluralistic culture, which highly values a certain form of tolerance, the controversy continues. Exclusive and ultimate truth claims about Jesus Christ are not welcomed. However, the Bible, as God's inspired and inerrant Word, provides the fundamental way to see Jesus rightly and to understand correctly who he is.

Jesus' coming was promised throughout the Old Testament, and His virgin birth is not mythology but history. Jesus is the God-man, complete in His deity and perfect in His humanity. As God's Son, he came to save sinners, and he is the only way to God. We believe this because Jesus said so Himself (John 14:6). He died on a Roman cross and made a perfect sacrifice and atonement for the sins of the world (1 John 2:2). On the Sunday following His crucifixion, God raised Him from the dead. Jesus' resurrection is not fable or fiction but historical fact. It establishes, by tangible proof, Jesus' lordship over all things (Philippians 2:9-11; Colossians 1:18). Forty days following His resurrection, Jesus ascended back to heaven, where he is exalted at His Father's right hand (Acts 1:9-11; Hebrews 1:3). Jesus' story, however, is not yet complete. The Bible promises that Jesus will come again to this earth as "KING OF KINGS AND LORD OF LORDS" (Revelation 19:16).

John Knox said, "No one else holds or has held the place in the heart of the world which Jesus holds. Other gods have been as devoutly worshipped; no other man has been so devotedly loved.[1]" Augustine described Him as, "beauty ever ancient, ever new."[2] This is the Christ we will examine.

CHAPTER 1

THE UNFOLDING PORTRAIT OF MESSIAH IN THE OLD TESTAMENT

No person has ever impacted the world like Jesus. C. S. Lewis captures something of the impact Jesus made when he came on the historical scene. In *Mere Christianity* he writes:

Among these Jews there suddenly turns up a man who goes about talking as if he was God. He claims to forgive sins. He says he has always existed. He says he is coming to judge the world at the end of time. Now let us get this clear. Among Pantheists, like the Indians, anyone might say that he was a part of God, or one with God: there would be nothing very odd about it. But this man, since he was a Jew, could not mean that kind of God. God, in their language, meant the Being outside the world who had made it and was infinitely different from anything else. And when you have grasped that, you will see that what this man said was, quite simply, the most shocking thing that has ever been uttered by human lips.[3]

Jesus indeed shocked the world. He did and said things that forced persons to make a decision about him. Who you think Jesus is becomes an inescapable question demanding an answer. Lewis is again helpful as he helps us narrow the legitimate options that are available.

I am trying here to prevent anyone saying the really fool-ish thing that people often say about him: "I'm ready to accept Jesus as a great moral teacher, but I don't accept his claim to be God." That is the one thing we must not say. A man who was merely a man and said the sort of things Jesus said would not be a great moral teacher. He would either be a lunatic—on a level with the man who says he is a poached egg—or else he would be the Devil of Hell. You must make your choice. Either this man was, and is, the Son of God; or else a madman or something worse. You can shut him up for a fool, you can spit at him and kill him as a demon; or you can fall at his feet and call him Lord and God. But let us not come with any patronizing nonsense about his being a great human teacher. He has not left that open to us. He did not intend to.[4]

It is out of this statement that we have the famous "trilemma" concerning who Jesus is. He is Lord, liar or lunatic. Lewis was on to something. However, I would like to make a slight adjustment by adding one other possibility: legend. Thus, there are actually four possible answers to the question, "Who is Jesus?"

1. Liar—he was not who he said he was and he knew so.
2. Lunatic—he was not who he thought he was and he did not know it.
3. Legend—he was not who others later imagined him to be.
4. Lord—he was who he said he was and his life, death and resurrection prove it to be so.

If Jesus is not the Christ, the fulfillment of Old Testament promise and prophecy, and he knew it, he is a *liar* of the worst sort and we should scorn him and ignore him. If he was not who he thought he was, given his tragically deluded self-understanding, we should pity him and dismiss him as a *lunatic*. It is rather difficult, however, on this position, to explain his remarkable teaching. If he is just a *legend*, something of a heroic make-believe character along the lines of the ancient Hercules or our Santa Claus, we might admire the stories for their wonderful charm, but we would certainly not view this person as the most significant individual to walk the earth, much less worship him. But, if he is *Lord*, the Son of God, the Messiah, the risen, ascended and exalted King of kings, we must decide what we will do with him.

The possibilities as to the identity of Jesus of Nazareth constitute divergent options. How one goes about the task of analyzing each is extremely crucial. We will start our study of Jesus with what I am calling a "Christology from behind." Here we start with the Old Testament, looking at what it says about the coming of a Messiah, a Savior. Whoever Jesus of Nazareth is, he did not appear in a vacuum. There was a historical context. There were hopes and expectations, especially on the part of Jewish persons, that God would intervene and remove the harsh and oppressive burden of Roman rule. The Old Testament greatly aids us in our attempt to answer the Jesus question and is an excellent place to begin.

The Old Testament's Redemptive and Messianic Storyline[5]

Genesis 3:15

The Old Testament is a "Messianic book," and the story of salvation begins in the Garden of Eden. Adam and Eve disobeyed God and plunged all of creation into sin (Genesis 3; Romans 8:19–23). Immediately God took the initiative to remedy the situation. In Genesis 3:15 God gives us the first promise of redemption, the *Protoevangelium,* the first gospel proclamation. God addresses the serpent, controlled and used by Satan (Romans 16:20), and says, "I will put hostility between you and the woman, and between your seed and her seed. He will strike your head, and you will strike his heel."

God promised that a male offspring of the woman would come and crush the serpent. He will conquer the evil one and restore to humanity what was forfeited when humans disobeyed God in the garden. This deliverer would come from the seed of woman. This text could be an implicit reference to the virgin birth of Jesus?

Genesis 12:1–3

Cain killed Abel (Genesis 4), and the world became so evil God destroyed it in a flood (Genesis 6–8). God then covenanted with Noah never to destroy the earth again by flood (Genesis 9), but the earth again turned away from the Lord at the tower of Babel (Genesis 11). At this point, the whole earth was filled with pride and rebellion. God, however, is faithful even when we are not, and he called a man and formed a nation through whom he would bless the earth and send his deliverer. God spoke to a man named Abram (Genesis 12:1-3).

Abram gave birth to a nation, the nation of Israel. By this man and through his descendents God would bless "all the peoples on earth." Abram, later called Abraham, meaning "father of many" (Genesis 17:5), would be the means by which God would bless the whole world.

Genesis 49:9–10

God kept his word and through Isaac and Jacob the descendants of Abraham grew, multiplied and landed in Egypt. As he neared death, Jacob gathered his sons around him and gave a "prophetic poem" (Genesis 49:2–27) telling them what would be in their future. His words about Judah are of particular importance and begin to narrow the specific line by which God would bless the whole world. The text reads:

You are a lion's cub, O Judah . . . The scepter will not depart from Judah, nor the ruler's staff from between his feet, until he comes to whom it belongs and the obedience of the nations is his (Genesis 49:9–10, *NIV*).

The thrust of the text points to the coming of a deliverer, a Messiah. It tells us he will come from the tribe of Judah and that he will be a king.

Deuteronomy 18:15

Moses adds a prophetic dimension to this unfolding portrait of the coming One. In Deuteronomy 18:15 he writes, "The Lord your God will raise up for you a prophet like me from among your own brothers. You must listen to him." From the greater context of this passage, it is clear that a series of prophets would be raised up by God to follow Moses. Yet, he does say, "a prophet like me," and it is interesting to note that in Israel's history the nation began to look and hope for "A Prophet," one associated with the Messiah. By the time of the New Testament, this was clearly the expectation (John 1:21, 45; 6:14; 7:40; Acts 3:20–22; 7:37).

2 Samuel 7:1–29

This chapter records the Lord's great promise to his servant King David. Next to Moses, no one in the Old Testament is held in higher esteem. And no one received a greater promise from God. Verses 9–14 delineate the specific promises God made to David in what is called the "Davidic Covenant:"

1. "I will make your name great, like the names of the greatest men of the earth" (7:9).
2. "I will establish a house (royal dynasty) for you" (7:11).
3. "I will establish the kingdom of your offspring (7:12) and the throne of his kingdom forever" (7:13).
4. "I will be his Father, and he will be my son" (7:14).
5. "I will never take my love away from him" (7:15).
6. "Your house and your kingdom will endure forever

before me; your throne will be established forever"
(7:16).

God commits himself to one of Abraham and
Judah's descendants in order to fulfill his promises
to Adam (Genesis 3:15), Abraham (Genesis 12:1–3)
and Judah (Genesis 49:9–10). By means of an un-
conditional covenant (note the repeated "I will's"),
God promises to establish an eternal Davidic dynasty. One must be careful when interpreting this text,
for it is a classic example of a prophecy with a dual
fulfillment, with both a near and a far focus. Immediately David's son Solomon is in view as the one
who will continue the Davidic monarchy following
David's death. He is the one to build the temple,
and God will punish him when he sins. The prophecy also has a distant fulfillment as verse 16 clearly
indicates when it speaks of a throne that will be established forever. This promise now becomes a major focal point of Messianic hope and expectation.
A future descendent of David will come and reign as
Israel's Messianic King. Encapsulating the promises

made to Abraham and Judah, he will be a blessing to the whole earth and also a sovereign King.

The Psalms

The Psalms are fertile soil in helping us fill out the details of God's coming deliverer. Psalms categorized as Messianic include Psalms 2, 18, 20, 45, 72, 89 and 110. There is also the incredible psalm of lament, Psalm 22. So striking is it in its similarity to the crucifixion of Jesus that many have referred to it as the "crucifixion psalm." There is also Psalm 16 and its promise of life beyond the grave.

Psalm 2. A royal Psalm composed perhaps for the coronation of a Davidic king, who is called the Lord's "Anointed One" (i.e. Messiah). Listen to what God says about this king:

"You are my Son; today I have become your Father."

And again in verse 12:

"Kiss the Son, lest he be angry and you be destroyed in your way."

This king is a Son who will rule not just Israel but the nations (2:8–9). All are called to kiss (submit to) him. Though Davidic kings in the past could have celebrated their coronation in this psalm, it looks beyond these kings to God's eschatological King, his Anointed One who will rule over David's house forever. VanGemeren notes,

> The first-century Church applied the second psalm to the Messiah as an explanation of the crucifixion of Christ by the rulers (Herod and Pontius Pilate), the nations, and Israel (the priests, scribes and Pharisees). They had conspired together against the Messiah of God (Acts 4:25–28). Paul applied it to Jesus ministry: his sonship, resurrection, and ascension to glory, which confirmed God's promises in Jesus as the Messiah (Acts 13:22–33).[6]

Psalm 16. This prayer song expresses confidence

and trust in God both in life and death. Verses 10–11 are crucial in their expression of hope beyond the grave:

> You will not abandon me to the grave (Hebrew Sheol), nor will you let your Holy One see decay. You have made known to me the path of life; you fill me with joy in your presence, with eternal pleasures in your right hand (NIV).

This psalm of prayer is also a psalm of prophecy. David is confident in the provisions of the Lord, including the provision of resurrection or deliverance from the grave for God's Holy One. Kidner is correct when he writes, "at its full value… this language is too strong even for David's hope of his own resurrection."[7] If not David, then who? The New Testament applied this psalm to Jesus (Acts 2).

Psalm 22. Spurgeon called Psalm 22, "the Psalm of the Cross." A psalm of lament, it is properly applied first to King David. However, the words of anguish of the godly sufferer in the psalm far transcends any experience of David. There will be a righteous sufferer who will be forsaken by God (22:1–2). He will suffer spiritually as well as physically. He will experience spiritual separation (22:1–2), verbal scorn (22:6–8), personal solitude (22:9–11), bodily suffering (22:12–16), and personal shame (22:17–18). Yet in spite of his great loss, God's servant rests in the confidence of God's deliverance (22:19–21). He is certain that God will allow him to again proclaim the Lord's name (22:22) even to the ends of the earth (22:27). Kidner says, "No Christian can read [Psalm 22] without being vividly confronted with the crucifixion. It is not only a matter of prophecy minutely fulfilled [note in particular 22:1, 6–9, 14–18], but of the sufferer's humility—there is no plea for vengeance—and his vision of a world-wide ingathering of the Gentiles."[8] Here is the prediction of God's righteous sufferer being crucified 1,000 years in advance, and several hundred years before the Medes and the Persians would even invent this torturous and inhumane method of execution![9] You read Psalm 22, and you would almost think you were reading Matthew 27, Mark 15, Luke 23, or John 19.

Psalm 110. No psalm is more clearly Messianic than this king-priest hymn. It bears the marks of a coronation psalm for the Davidic king, but the language transcends any ancient king of Israel. So lofty and exalted is the language that the Hebrew people viewed it as speaking of Messiah, even before the Christian era. Two verses in particular stand out:

The LORD says to my Lord: "Sit at my right hand until I make your enemies a footstool for your feet." (Psalm 110:1)

The LORD has sworn and will not change his mind: "You are a priest forever in the order of Melchizedek." (Psalm 110:4)

Several important observations arise from these two verses. First, *Yahweh* gives to David's Lord authority over all his enemies in words that recall the glory and honor given to God's anointed in Psalm 2. Second, it makes this Davidic king a co-regent with *Yahweh* (Psalm 89:27). Third, because of this declaration by the LORD, victory for this Davidic ruler will "extend from Zion against all the enemies" (110:2-3).[10] Fourth, this Davidic ruler will be a "king-priest," but one of a completely unique order. On rare occasions a king from Israel functioned temporarily as a priest (2 Samuel 6:13–17). More often they were rebuked and punished for usurping an assignment that was not theirs (Saul in 1 Samuel 13:8–15 and Uzziah in 2 Kings 15; 2 Chronicles 26:19–21).[11] This king-priest is different. The LORD invokes an oath whereby his priesthood is established. Further, he is to be a priest forever. Finally, his order is not that of Aaron, but of the ancient and mysterious king-priest Melchizedek (Genesis 14:17–20). A Davidic King is coming who will rule victoriously as both king and priest, defeat all enemies, and reign forever.

Isaiah 7:14

Isaiah is the most significant book among the prophets concerning the coming of Messiah. Texts like Isaiah 7:14, 9:6–7, 11:1–16, and the Servant

Songs of 42:1–7, 49:1–6, 50:4–9, 52:13–53:12 further develop the portrait the Lord paints as redemptive history unfolds.

Isaiah 7:14 is another example of an Old Testament prophecy with a dual fulfillment, a near and far aspect. Ahaz's rejection of the Lord (7:10–12) will bring judgment upon him and an apparent end to the Davidic dynasty (7:2). However, God will remain faithful to David. This promise is found in the "Immanuel" prophecy (meaning "God with us") of 7:14. In some mysterious and sovereign act, a divine-human Messiah will appear. If Ahaz will not ask for a sign (7:12), God will give him one anyway:

> The virgin will be with child and will give birth to a son,
> and will call him Immanuel. (7:14)

The word "virgin" is important. It is the Hebrew word *almah*. This word is more fluid and ambiguous than another Hebrew word, *betulah*, which always refers to a virgin. *Almah* means simply, "a young woman of marriageable age." While the word does not demand that the woman in view is a virgin, the idea would naturally be present in the Hebrew culture of the day.[12] However, it is the ambiguity of *almah* that allows for the near fulfillment in Isaiah's day and a far, future, eschatological fulfillment in Jesus! Oswalt is helpful and writes,

> The conclusion to which we are driven is that while the prophet [under divine inspiration] did not want to stress the virginity, neither did he wish to leave it aside... Possibly, then, it is the dual focus of the oracle that explains the use of álmâ here. In the short term, the virgin conception does not seem to have had primary importance. Rather, the significance is that a child conceived at that moment would still be immature when the two threatening nations would have been destroyed (verses 16, 22).[13]

Still there is something more. A child born in Ahaz's day, whether his own or one born to Isaiah, is not a sign of God's continuing presence. But, as Oswalt adds,

If a virgin overshadowed by God's Spirit should conceive and give birth, it would not only be a sign of God's presence with us. Better than that, it would be the reality of that experience. So Ahaz's sign must be rooted in its own time to have significance for that time, but it also must extend beyond that time and into a much more universal mode if its radical truth is to be any more than a vain hope.[14]

The mother will call him Immanuel, for in him God will uniquely be in the midst of his people. But how? Chapter 9 provides the answer.

Isaiah 9:6–7

This text introduces us to the King with four names. The passage is also an extension of the "virgin conception/Immanuel prophecy" of Isaiah 7:14. The time is somewhere around 725 BC. The northern kingdom of Israel faces an ominous situation. From the north, Tiglath Pileser III has built Assyria into a military machine. Now Shalmaneser V is poised to attack a morally and militarily weakened Israel. Israel would be invaded, sacked, overrun and crushed in humiliating defeat in 722 BC. A proud nation would be brought to its knees in shame and humiliation. And yet, in the midst of their despair and hopelessness, a word of hope arrives. The gloom, distress, humiliation, darkness, and death of 9:1–2 would be turned into the rejoicing, joy, light, liberation, and peace of 9:2–5. How? By the coming of the King with four names. E. J. Young nicely paraphrases the hope that springs out of the despair of their immediate circumstances:

> There is great rejoicing among God's people, because God has broken the yoke of burden and oppression, and the burden and oppression are removed because the weapons and garments of the warrior are destroyed, and the basic reason for these blessings is that a Child is born. In contrast to the mighty foe of Assyria and also to the Syro-Ephraimitic coalition, a Child brings deliverance to the people of God.[15]

The language is precise and enticing: "For unto us a child is born, to us a son is given." This child is the same as the child of 7:14. There his birth was a sign; here it is the very means of deliverance and salvation![16]

This Davidic ruler is now described in terms that carry Messianic hope to an entirely new level. "A child will be born" emphasizes his humanity. "A son will be given" emphasizes what? Dare we conclude that "the expected perfect king will be human and divine"?[17] Government will rest on this child. He will be a king, a ruler, and a sovereign lord. But look at his titles! These are not normal titles. "Wonderful Counselor" is literally "wonder of a counselor." This divine deliverer is wondrous and unfathomable in his wisdom. "Mighty God" is striking. Such a bold declaration causes some to see it as "an example of popular hyperbole."[18] Such a reading is untrue to the plain meaning of the text, startling though it is. "Mighty God" (Hebrew *el gibbor*) is always used in the Old Testament as a reference to God (10:21; also Deuteronomy 10:17; Jeremiah 32:18).[19] This text is a clear and direct affirmation of Messiah's deity. "Everlasting Father" is as striking as mighty God. It tells us something about the character of Messiah and his relationship to his people. He is fatherly in his compassion, concern, and love for them. This fatherly love is eternal. "Prince of peace" is appropriate as a concluding title. He is a king who brings peace: peace between man and man, as well as peace between God and man. Is it possible that this could be accomplished except by one who is himself God?

Verse 7 is clearly eschatological in focus. This King "will be the final king, the king to end all kings."[20] Of his government and peace there will be no end. He will reign as the Messianic heir to David's throne (2 Samuel 7:12–16) forever. All of it is certain to come to pass for "the zeal of the LORD Almighty will accomplish this" (9:7). The Messiah will be a great king, a world Savior, and a harbinger of peace. But what is the means whereby his kingdom will come to be established? Psalm 22 gave us a hint, but who could have imagined God's Messiah would be a "SERVANT KING?"

Isaiah 52:13–53:12

The text introduces us to "the Suffering Servant of the Lord." It is the fourth of the Great Servant Songs of Isaiah (42:1–7; 49:1–6; 50:4–9). The twin themes of *exaltation* and *humiliation* are woven throughout.

The Servant in view is Messiah, the royal Davidic King, the *ideal* Israelite. He embodies all that is good in Israel. The picture of the Servant of the Lord, of his mission to Israel and to the world, and of his substitutionary suffering, is prophecy of the future. Philip the evangelist in Acts 8:35 makes plain to the man from Ethiopia that the Suffering Servant is Jesus, and Isaiah 53 is directly cited no less than seven times in the New Testament and with more than forty allusions. Jesus, in Mark 10:45, weds Isaiah's Suffering Servant to Daniel's Son of Man (Daniel 7:13–14) and thereby redefines for us who and what Messiah will be.

Now, what does this text tell us about the Servant of the Lord? The list is staggering. He bore our grief (53:4). He carried our sorrows (53:4). He was wounded for our transgressions (53:5). He was bruised for our iniquities (53:5). He was chastised for our peace (53:5). He healed us by his stripes (53:5). He bore our iniquities (53:6, 11). He was oppressed and afflicted (53:7). He was slaughtered (53:7). He was cut off (53:8). He was stricken for our transgressions (53:8). He was bruised by the Lord (53:10). He was put to grief (53:10). His soul was made a sin offering (53:10). He poured out his soul to death (53:12). He was numbered with the transgressors (53:12). He bore the sin of many (53:12). He made intercession for the transgressors (53:12).

The messianic hope is a single line that begins in broadest terms with God's promise of victory over the serpent through "the seed of woman" (Genesis 3:15), then it narrows successively to the seed of Abraham (Genesis 22:18), the tribe of Judah (Genesis 49:10), the stem of Jesse (Isaiah 11:1), the house/dynasty of David (2 Samuel 7) and finally the suffering and slain servant of Yahweh (Isaiah 53). However, the portrait is not complete. We now move to Daniel 7.

Daniel 7:13–14

Here the mysterious "Son of Man" is introduced. This text is the only overt reference in the Old Testament to the Messiah as the Son of Man. The language of these verses is reminiscent of Genesis 1:28; 2 Samuel 7:12–16; Psalm 2; 8; and Isaiah 9:7. The one described as "like a son of man" has the appearance of a man, but he is much more than a mere mortal. He comes with the clouds, a sign of deity in the ancient world. He is given the rule over all things, coronated by the "Ancient of Days," God himself. He is to be worshiped and his kingdom is everlasting. This final eschatological Ruler is not just a man; he is "the heavenly Sovereign incarnate."[21] That Daniel 7:13–14 speaks of Messiah is a view that dates back to early Jewish, and of course Christian, interpreters. Rabbinic interpreters and the Talmud saw the one described in these verses as God's Messiah.[22] That he would partake of characteristics and honor that are both human and divine no doubt would have mystified the initial Hebrew readers.

Micah 5:2

A day of judgment is on Jerusalem's horizon (Micah 5:1). However, a promised deliverer will appear from the tiny and insignificant town of Bethlehem. He "will be ruler over Israel," and amazingly, "his goings out are from old, from days of eternity." Is there again a hint that Messiah will be divine, that he is a preexistent person? He is born a baby in Bethlehem, but is he also one who has existed from days of eternity.

There is no question the Old Testament picture of Messiah is mysterious and complex, but step-by-step God reveals to us who the deliverer would be and what the deliverer would do. Kaiser is correct when he says, "The OT writers did consciously and knowingly write and point to the Messiah as being a special son born in the line of David, with the special divine nature that belonged to God alone."[23]

This, then, is what we should look for. This is what we will find in Jesus of Nazareth, a 1st century Jew and God's Messiah-Son.

CHAPTER 2

FULLY DIVINE/FULLY HUMAN

Biblical Christology recognizes no distinction between the Jesus who actually lived, the Jesus reported in the Gospels, and the Jesus of the epistles The Jesus of history and the Christ of faith are one and the same. Jesus Christ is fully God and fully man. This truth has been universally accepted by the Church as the orthodox/biblical position at least until the modern era. Marcus Borg is a good example of the modernistic perspective. He says, "An older, doctrinal understanding of Christianity has ceased to be persuasive. There's been an appetite for looking at Jesus in a way that doesn't depend on Christian theological claims such as Jesus is the only begotten son of God."[24]

The witness of the Bible is that God indeed became one of us in the person of Jesus Christ. The Old Testament promised that he would come, and the New Testament testifies he came. The Word (God the Son) became flesh (John 1:14). Four texts stand out in what they teach concerning both the deity and humanity of Jesus. The texts are John 1:1-18, Philippians 2:5-11, Colossians 1:15-23; 2:9-10, and Hebrews 1:1-4. They provide for us a "heaven's-eye" viewpoint of Jesus. Here we discover "Christology from above."[25]

John 1:1-18 – The God of Incarnation

The Prologue of John

Modern persons often have difficulty with the deity of Christ. Persons in the 1st century actually had difficulty with his humanity as well. John's prologue (1:1-18) addresses both in a balanced manner. There is a clear affirmation of Christ's deity (Colossians

1-2; Philippians 2; and Hebrews 1-2). He is the *Logos* (revelation/communication) of God; the Life (creation/salvation) of God; and the Light (salvation/revelation) of God. The importance of John 1:14 can scarcely be overemphasized: "The Word became flesh and took up residence among us." In addition, John elsewhere emphasizes the Son's unique relationship to the Father and provides the most significant material in Scripture for the development of the doctrine of the Trinity. This relationship is demonstrated in the Upper Room Discourse in John 14-16. Here a number of important themes are expressed: 1) the essential oneness of the Father and the Son (14:9-10); 2) the distinctiveness of persons within the Godhead (14:16-18); and 3) the functional subordination of the Son to the Father (14:24, 31; 16:5, 28). John's Gospel is a gold mine for Christological reflection.

Jesus: the Logos of God

Jesus is called the Word or *Logos* in John 1:1, 14. *Logos* is a word with a rich and varied history. Potential sources for John's concept include Palestinian Judaism, Greek Philosophy, Hellenistic (Greek influenced) Judaism, and the Old Testament. John utilizes *Logos* because of its capacity to communicate to multiple cultures. He uses it for the purpose of missions and evangelism. The term was well known, but John fills it with "new meaning." The Greek philosopher Philo believed *Logos* was "reason" and an "it." John's *Logos* is "the Word" and a "He." Philo's *Logos* was a principle. John's *Logos* is a person. John's *Logos* is not only God's agent in creation; He is God. He is God's personal, visible (1:14) communication to man. *Logos* does not explain Jesus; Jesus explains and fills with new meaning *Logos*. Wisdom has become a person. Divine reason has become a man.

The Greeks were correct in affirming we could not reach the *Logos*. John informs us that we need not despair. The *Logos* came down and lived among us.

To the Greeks *Logos* is reason. To the Jews *Logos* is the Word/wisdom. In John, these ideas find new meaning as they are embodied in a person: Jesus Christ.

Theological Truths Gleaned from the Prologue

John establishes the preexistence of the Word in eternity past: "In the beginning was the *Logos*" (1:1). The *Logos* already "was" when the beginning took place. Furthermore, this *Logos* was "face to face with" God, indicating a distinction of persons within the Godhead, as well as an equality of persons. There was never a time when the *Logos* was not fully God. Indeed he is affirmed as being: 1) coequal, 2) co-eternal, 3) coexistent and 4) consubstantial with the Father.

In verse three John affirms that not a single thing that exists came into being except through him. That he created all things logically and necessarily leads to the conclusion that he himself is not created. The importance of this theological proposition cannot be too strongly emphasized. F. F. Bruce notes, "When heaven and earth were created, there was the Word of God, already existing in the closest association with God and partaking of the essence of God. No matter how far back we may try to push our imagination, we can never reach a point at which we could say of the Divine Word, as Arius did, 'There once was when He was not.'"[26] Join this with the fact that a Jew like the apostle John would only know the God of Genesis 1-2 as the Creator, and you have further evidence of the full deity of Jesus.

Perhaps some type of incipient Gnosticism, or better, Docetism, necessitates John 1:14. Gnosticism, from the Greek word *gnosis* meaning knowledge, teaches that salvation is by mystical knowledge and that the material world is inferior or evil. Docetism, from *dokeo* (meaning "to appear"), says Christ was some type of phantom or mystical spirit who did not have a real, physical body. Both false teachings denied the genuine and permanent reality of the incarnation whereby God took to himself real humanity. John insists that the Word is not only truly God, he has also become truly human. John teaches that our

Lord was tired and thirsty (4:6-7); he wept (11:35); he was troubled in spirit (12:17; 13:21), and he bled and died (19:30). Without becoming less than God (Philippians 2:5-11), the Son took upon himself complete humanity apart from sin (2 Corinthians 5:21; Hebrews 4:15). John affirms "He became flesh." At his incarnation, God did not become man; he became God-Man. The words "dwelt among us" can be understood to mean Jesus "pitched his tent" or "tabernacle" among us. Just as the Hebrew *shekinah* ("glory"), the bright cloud of God's glorious person settled upon the tabernacle (Exodus 24:16; 40:35), even so in Christ God's glorious person dwelt among men and they beheld, gazed upon and examined his glory.[27] The one who was from all eternity was in the most intimate and personal relationship with the Father and has "exegeted," declared, explained and made known the Father (1:18). So if we desire to be theologically precise, we can say there was a time when Jesus was not. However, there was never a time when the Son was not.

Philippians 2:5-11 – The God of Humiliation

This beautiful passage is one of the New Testament "Christ hymns," which provide insight into the theology and worship of the Early Church[28] Philippians 2 is especially noted for two important aspects of Christology: 1) The *kenosis doctrine* or "emptying of Christ," as God the Son became a man, and 2) the *hypostatic union* (the uniting of two natures in one person).

The hymn appears in two stanzas: A) stanza 1 (verses 6-8) show *Christ's humiliation*; and B) stanza 2 (verses 9-11) show *Christ's exaltation.* Interestingly, the hymn of 2:6-11 actually serves as an illustration (and a divine one at that!) of the mind of Christ (2:5); the mind believers should pursue and cultivate.

For Paul, like John, the starting point of the hymn is "the preexistence of Christ." Philippians 2:6 reads: "who, existing in the form of God." "Existing" emphasizes continued existence. Christ has always existed. He existed in the realm of eternity, forever. He always is (John 8:58). There never was a time when

he was not. He is eternally existent. By definition this would mean he is God. The word translated "form" is *morphe*. This word has been variously understood. Opinion includes: 1) the essential nature and character of God; 2) the mode of being or way of being 3) the image of God; and 4) the glory of God. Th four options are similar to each other, and each high lights a truth about Jesus taught in the Bible. Still v should do our best to "get at" the precise idea Pa was teaching.

A word study of *morphe* is a good place to sta *Morphe* identifies Jesus with the essential nature a character of God. The idea is that of an "outw display of an inner reality or substance." Christ e nally exists in the very nature, essence, essentia ing, and glory of God. Whatever characteristics n God, Christ is, in all of God's glory! *Morphe* (fc denotes Christ as being the permanent uncha able pattern of deity. However, Christ "did not sider equality with God as something to be use His own advantage" (verse 6). This phrase look to the expression existing in the form of God

Son's equal status and privileges with God were not things that he violently sought to seize or believed he must forcibly retain. "Grasped" (HCSB marginal reading) is *harpagmos* (Greek), and can mean 1) robbing (active sense) or 2) a prize gained through robbery (passive sense).[29] Being co-equal and co-eternal with God by the very nature of his being, equality with God was not something Christ had to forcibly strive for (as if he did not possess it) or assert (as if he could lose it). Bruce notes,

> There is no question of Christ's trying to snatch or seize equality with God: that was already his because he always had the nature of God. Neither is there any question of his trying to retain it by force. The point is rather that he did not treat his equality with God as an excuse for self-assertion or self-aggrandizement; on the contrary, he treated it as an occasion for renouncing every advantage or privilege that might have accrued to him thereby, as an opportunity for self-impoverishment and unreserved self-sacrifice.[30]

Some students of Scripture have seen a contrast here with Adam: Christ enjoyed true equality with God but refused to derive any advantage from it in becoming man, whereas Adam, a man made in the image of God, snatched at a false and illusory equality. Christ achieved universal lordship through his renunciation, whereas Adam forfeited his lordship through his "snatching." If a Christ/Adam contrast is in Paul's mind, a comparison of the two is certainly enlightening.

ADAM AND CHRIST:
Comparison and Contrast

ADAM	CHRIST
1) Made in the divine image.	1) Was and is the very essence of God.
2) Thought it a prize to be grasped to be as God.	2) Thought it not a prize to be grasped to be as God.
3) Aspired to a reputation.	3) Made Himself of no reputation.
4) Spurned being God's servant.	4) Took upon Himself the form (*morphe*) of a servant (slave).
5) Sought to be in the very likeness of God.	5) Was made in the likeness of men.
6) Being found in fashion as a man, exalted himself and became disobedient unto death.	6) Being found in fashion as a man (Romans 8:3), humbled himself and became obedient unto death.
7) Was condemned and disgraced.	7) Was highly exalted by God and given the name and position of Lord.

Adam was humanity seeking deity. Christ was deity seeking humanity. Christ grasped not at sovereignty but service. Christ did not grasp. Christ gave. He did not climb; He condescended.

Philippians 2:7-8 says, "He emptied Himself." The crucial word is *kenoō* (Greek), meaning simply "to empty." Verses 7-8 express a clear and straightforward understanding of what it means that Christ's "made himself of no reputation." He assumed the form (*morphe*) of a servant (*doulos*, Greek). He took on the likeness and external form of a man. He humbled himself (verses 2-4). He became obedient to the point of death. He died a cross-type of death. There was an emptying by addition. The Son did not surrender his deity; He added humanity. Further, the type of humanity he added was not that of a sovereign, but that of a servant/slave. He received not a crown, but a cross. Bruce again says it well: "It was in the manner of his death, his death on the cross, that the rock bottom of humiliation was reached... By the standards of the first century, no experience could be more loathsomely degrading than that."[31] However, deity cannot cease to be deity, so any understanding of *keneo* ("to empty") that would point in this direction must quickly be dismissed.

Yet, a real and genuine emptying took place. John 17:5 is helpful here. Here our Lord says, "Now, Father, glorify Me in your presence with the glory I had with You before the world existed." Jesus did not surrender his deity, but he did surrender his glory. He became in a sense "God incognito." The wedding of deity and humanity was permanent. The emptying, however, was only for the time of incarnation. Christ temporarily laid aside the free and voluntary exercise of the rights and privileges of deity! The emptying therefore involved self-limitation as well as ultimate humiliation. Christ partook of unglorified humanity. He voluntarily forfeited, for a time, the free use of his divine attributes, depending instead on his Father and the Holy Spirit.

God, however, does not leave the drama unresolved. Jesus in humiliation totally reverses the priorities and values of this world system. His Father affirms his pleasure in his Son in the Son's exaltation. Verses 9-11 affirm a three-fold exaltation of the Savior: an exalted *position* (verse 9), an exalted *adoration* (verse 10), and an exalted *confession* (verse 11).

Philippians 2:9-11 notes the action of God the Father in light of the Son's voluntary obedience and humiliation. "Highly exalted" means to exalt above and beyond, to super exalt. No doubt Paul has in mind our

Lord's resurrection, ascension and present session in heaven. "Given him a name" may have reference to the name Yahweh, Lord, or Jesus. "Lord" seems more likely, though merit lies in all three options. The bowing of adoration (verse 10) and the word of confession (verse 11) serve to emphasize the deity and universal lordship of the Son, a reality that glorifies the Father.

Isaiah 45:23 is echoed in verse 10. In Isaiah, Yahweh is in view. In Philippians, it is Jesus. It is no accident that Jesus has ascribed to him that which is ascribed to the God of the Old Testament, for Jesus is God. All will bow (verse 10). Nothing in all of creation is outside of the Lordship and authority of the Lord Jesus Christ. Bruce notes,

> "Jesus (Christ) is Lord" is the quintessential Christian creed, and in that creed "Lord" is given the most august sense that it can bear. When Christians in later generations refused to say "Caesar is Lord," they refused because they knew that this was no more courtesy title that Caesar claimed: It was a title that implied his right to receive divine honors, and in this sense they give it to

none but Jesus. To them there was "only one God, the Father, ... and ... only one Lord, Jesus Christ" (1 Cor 8:6). In the Greek O.T. Gentile Christians read, Yahweh was denoted either by *theos* ("God") or (most often) by *kyrios* ("Lord"); they reserved *theos* regularly for God the Father and *kyrios* regularly for Jesus. When divine honors are thus paid to the humiliated and exalted Jesus, the glory of God the Father is not diminished but enhanced. When the Son is honored, the Father is glorified; for none can bestow on the Son higher honors than the Father himself has bestowed.[32]

Colossians 1:15-20 – The God of Creation

Colossians 1-2 has played a significant role in the battles that the Church has fought in the area of Christology. T. L. Trevethan writes, "The foundation of the argument of the letter to the Colossians is found in 2:9-10. The gospel, Christian truth, has its source in Jesus. He is the crown of God's revelation because 'in him the whole fullness of deity dwells bodily' (Colossians 2:9). There is no stronger statement of the full deity of our Lord Jesus in the Scripture."[33] Bruce adds, "This is one of the great Christological passages of the New Testament, declaring as it does our Lord's divine essence, pre-existence, and creative agency."[34] As a statement of Christology Colossians 2:9-10, along with 1:15-20, scarcely has a superior.

These verses are a "Christ Hymn" exalting the Son as the supreme Lord.[35] Verse 15 begins with the affirmation that Christ is the "image (*eikon*) of the invisible God" (2 Corinthians 4:4), a word meaning likeness, representation, image, form, manifestation, and reflection. It implies the outward manifestation and illumination of something's *inner core* and essence. Here and in 2 Corinthians 4:4, this word is used of a precise and absolute correspondence. Jesus Christ is the perfect visible manifestation of the invisible God. He is the perfect expression and representation of God the Father. John Calvin provides a valuable commentary when he writes,

> [Paul] calls Him the *image of the invisible God*, meaning by this, that it is in him alone that God, who is otherwise invisible, is manifested to us.... Christ is called the *image of God*

on this ground – that He makes God in a manner visible to us…. We must, therefore, beware of seeking Him [God] elsewhere, for everything that would set itself off as a representation of God apart from Christ, will be an idol.[36]

Adam may have been created *in* God's image, but Christ *is* God's image. He brings to light and makes knowable the God who, both to our physical and inward eyes, is invisible. Jesus is the person and "portrait of God."[37]

Jesus himself said, "The one who has seen me has seen the Father" (John 14:9), and "before Abraham was, I am" (John 8:58, Exodus 3:14). Colossians 1:15 also is an explicit affirmation of Christ's divine essence. Paul is affirming Christ as Lord God, both of the cosmos (his material creation) and the Church (his spiritual creation).

Christ is Lord of Creation (1:15-17)

Christ is called the firstborn (Greek *prototokos*). "Firstborn" obviously has the nuance of supremacy and preeminence from the expressions that follow in verses 16-17. Christ is the source-agent and preserver of creation and is worthy of all worship. Christ as sustainer ("by Him all things hold together") makes the universe a cosmos instead of a chaos. *Prototokos* is used twice here because of its emphasis upon the divine preeminence of Jesus as the Lord of his universal creation. Christ is the Creator, preeminent over every creature. A Jew, such as Paul, could only conceive of God as Creator. Further, since Christ created "all things," he himself must be uncreated or the statement is untrue. The Son is not God's greatest creation through whom all else came into existence. He is the Creator, and by him all that is came into existence. Christ is God. He is preexistent and preeminent over all creation as its God.

Christ Is the Lord of the Church (1:18-20)

Christ also is the head of the body (verse 18), the Church. The Church owes him exclusive allegiance, complete devotion, and total obedience. The pronoun ("he") is emphatic, meaning Christ, and no other, is head. He alone is its Lord and ruler.

Notice again the term "firstborn" in verse 18b: "He is the beginning, the firstborn from the dead." Beginning may mean: 1) supremacy in rank, 2) precedence in time, or 3) creative initiative. All three ideas are true, though creative initiative seems to be the idea Paul intends to convey.[38] Here *prototokos* has to do with the fact that he conquered death in his resurrection. He is sovereign even over death. His resurrection is his claim to be head of the Church.

Christ has full rights over the Church because he conquered the great enemy of his people: death. In so doing, he proved himself to be God! Hence, verse 18 sums up the matter: Christ should "have first place in everything!"

Verse 19 explains that in Christ we see the very essence of God. "All the fullness" means that Christ lacks nothing of what it means to be God (e.g., saving grace, love, goodness, light, omniscience, etc.). The word "fullness" was possibly a technical term in the vocabulary of false teachers. Paul uses this word eight times in this letter. It has the sense of something being "undiluted" or "unalloyed." Christ is "pure deity," and "nothing of deity is lacking in Christ."[39]

By linking Christ's deity with his incarnation in the word "bodily," Paul makes clear that Christ is fully God and fully man. This verse (19) is, along with 2:9-10, one of the New Testament's best verses to show both Christ's deity and Christ's humanity, as well as to show that he is both fully God and fully man *at the same time.*

The God of Revelation – Hebrews 1:1-4

An old puritan preacher said there were only two things he needed to know: 1) Does God speak? 2) What does God say? To these two excellent questions I would add a third: 3) Is Jesus God's final word? I believe we find the answer to all three of these questions in Hebrews 1:1-4, a fourth major Christological text.

Hebrews has an overriding theme in its 13 chapters: Jesus is God's very best. The word "better" or "superior" occurs 19 times in the New Testament, 13 of those in Hebrews. Here we discover that Jesus:

1. Is better than the angels. (1:4)
2. Provides a better hope. (7:19)
3. Provides a better covenant. (7:22; 8:6)
4. Provides better promises. (8:6)
5. Provides a better sacrifice. (9:23)
6. Provides a better possession. (10:34)
7. Provides a better country. (11:16)
8. Provides a better resurrection. (11:35)
9. Provides a better blood testimony. (12:24)

In the coming of Christ, God 1) speaks, 2) He speaks clearly, and 3) He speaks with finality.

God Has Spoken Decisively in His Son. (1:1-2)

Francis Schaeffer said, "The infinite personal God is there, but also he is not silent; that changes

the whole world."[40] The Christian God is a talking
God, and his revelation through his prophets was
true, though partial (1:1). At different times and in
different ways God spoke. Because it was God speaking, it was true. And, because it was in many portions
and in many ways, it was partial and progressive.
What he gave the fathers and prophets was inerrant
but incomplete. It was promise, not fulfillment.

God spoke through visions and dreams. He spoke
through angels, natural events, and pillars of fire.
He spoke in history, psalms, proverbs, and prophecy.
Yet according to his providential plan, it was partial,
step-by-step, elemental, and preparatory.

In contrast, God's revelation through his Son is
true and perfect (1:2). "Last days" speaks of the final
age, the messianic age, where we have been since the
cross. "Spoken" is the same word as in verse 1. The
same God spoke in both, but now there is a difference in time (the last days) and quality (through his
Son). Schaeffer says, "He is there and is not a silent,
nor [is he] a far off God."[41] God came near as he
spoke in his Son.

God Has Shown Himself Decisively in Jesus (1:2-3)

Jesus is the face of God! Jesus is the invisible God made visible! When you look at Jesus, you are looking at God. Now if you look closely, exactly what do you see? Hebrews provides seven glorious affirmations.

1. He is the divine inheritor (1:2). Christ has supreme place in all of creation. The Father delights to honor the Son. All things belong to him.

2. He is the divine creator (1:2). All three members of the triune God are active in creation. The Father is the author, the Son is the administrator, and the Holy Spirit is the agent. Here attention is on the Son. From Genesis to Revelation, from the Garden of Eden to the Island of Patmos, all of Scripture and all of history are about Jesus.

3. He is the divine revealer (1:3). In Jesus, the Son, we see the true and authentic glory of God. As the sunlight is to the sun, so the eternal Son is to the Father.[42]

4. He is the divine character (1:3). When you see Jesus you see who God really is. This is not true of any other person in history. Jesus Christ, God's Son, alone reveals to us exactly what the Father is like.

5. *He is the divine sustainer (1:3).* Through his powerful, enabling, active word he spoke the worlds into existence, and by that same word he sustains the worlds until their proper end.

6. *He is the divine redeemer (1:3).* Jesus did what no forefather or prophet could ever do. He did what no apostle or angel could ever do. He did what only he could do: he took care of our sin. Purification is *katharismos* (Greek). It means to cleanse, purge, or purify. Jesus cleansed us of sins (1:4); He made a satisfaction for sins (2:17); He puts away sins (8:12; 10:17); He bore our sins (9:28); he offered a sacrifice for sins for all times (10:12); He made an offering for sins (10:18), and He annulled sin by his sacrifice (9:26). Look at sin any way you will—he has dealt with it. He has defeated it.[43] We needed a spiritual catharsis, a divine cleansing. Jesus accomplished that.

7. *He is the divine savior (1:3).* Unlike any high priest under the old covenant, Jesus' atonement work is finished. Jesus rests in the position of greatest honor because his work of atonement is over.

God Is Rightly Honored in the Worship of Jesus (1:4)

The Bible is clear: there is only one way to the Father. We come by way of the Son. This Son is to be exclusively worshipped, honored, and lifted up. Why?

1. Jesus is the Creator (1:4, 13-14). Angels are mentioned 105 times in the Old Testament and 165 in the New Testament. They are ministering spirits for the saved (1:14). They are good; they are not, however, the best. They are servants. Jesus is sovereign (1:7). They are creatures. Jesus is the Creator. They are workers. Jesus is worshipped (1:6).

2. Jesus is the exalted Son (1:4 ff.). Angels are called servants. Jesus is called Son. Angels continue to serve for God. Jesus is now seated by God. In all respects Jesus is better: better in his person (he is God), better in his work (he dealt with sin once and for all), and better in his position (he is at God's right hand). God has many servants, but only one Son. His name is Jesus.

CHAPTER 3

A Life Like No Other: A Survey of the Major Events in the Earthly Life of Jesus

The life of Jesus is a fascinating story. To understand the first century and the context out of which Christianity was born, you must examine this man. In his brief earthly life of approximately 33 years, a number of events stand out. They are historically important and theologically significant. Scripture provides testimony from eyewitnesses or those closely associated with these witnesses. In Luke's case, he had carefully investigated everything so that there could be a certainty about what had been taught (Luke 1:1–4).

When you read a statement like Luke's, it makes the skepticism of some modern persons unwarranted. For example, Peter Bien, professor of English at Dartmouth College and the translator of Nikos Kazantzakis' infamous *The Last Temptation of Christ* says,

> I don't think we know who Jesus was. The Gospels, which were written for political purposes—to convert people—are after the fact. Fifty years at least. Mary? Well, obviously he had a mother, so it had to be somebody—her name doesn't matter. Then one Gospel writer says he was born in Nazareth, the other says Bethlehem. Joseph might have been a shoemaker, not a carpenter. Some traditions said Jesus had brothers, others said Joseph had no other children. What difference does it make? The Gospel writers were novelists . . . I realize much of what we know about Jesus is novelistic. But I act as if it isn't.[44]

Or consider the even more skeptical and somewhat cynical judgment of deceased atheist Jon Murray, former president of American Atheist: "There was no such person in the history of the world as Jesus Christ. There was no historical, living breathing, sentient human being by that name. Ever. [The Bible] is a fictional, nonhistorical narrative. The myth is good for business."[45]

A fair and honest investigation of the Bible, however, reveals eyewitness testimony that fits well into the historical world of the first century. In this chapter we will pursue what theologians call a "Christology from below."

The Virgin Birth[46]

Its Importance

The virgin birth is critical to our understanding of the union of deity and humanity of Jesus. It teaches that God became man, and that there is no contradiction in the idea that God can take on a human nature. The virgin birth demonstrates that God is not so transcendent as to be "wholly other" and hence utterly unknowable to his creatures.

The Biblical Witness

Several key texts address the issue of the virgin birth:

1. Isaiah 7:14ff. (also 9:6–7; 11:1ff.)
2. Matthew 1:18–25
3. Luke 1:26–38
4. Genesis 3:15 (a veiled reference to be sure)
5. Possible allusions may also include Romans 1:3; 5:12–21; Galatians 4:4; Philippians 2:6.

Matthew examines the birth from Joseph's perspective and provides a legal genealogy back to David beginning in 1:1-17. Luke looks at the event from Mary's perspective and provides a natural genealogy, also back to David, in 3:23–38. The accounts are complementary to one another.

Matthew teaches us that Joseph was in no way involved in the conception of Jesus (1:25). He did have normal marital relations with Mary after Jesus was born (1:25), and he was responsible for the naming of the child (1:25). All of this was a fulfillment of the prophecy of the virgin birth in Isaiah 7:14 (1:22–23). The main point of the virgin conception is that it is a sign that God is again acting in the midst of his people.

Luke, on the other hand, emphasizes that Mary is a virgin (Matthew also has this emphasis), and that the event surprised her (1:29–30). Luke 1:35 shows that the Holy Spirit was the divine agent in the virginal conception. Emphasis is on the divine generation of Messiah by means of the Spirit.

In sum, the story of the virgin birth, or virgin conception, is prophesied in Isaiah 7:14 and described in the infancy narratives of Matthew 1:18–25 and Luke 1:26–38. The biblical record reveals that Jesus Christ was born without a human father, conceived by the Holy Spirit, and born of the Virgin Mary.

Did the Virgin Birth Really Happen?

Most who reject the virgin birth claim that it is mythological. The idea of the Son of God assuming a human nature in the womb of a virgin too closely parallels ancient myths and legends. Robert Stein says, "Probably the most frequent argument raised against the virginal conception is that too many other parallels exist in ancient literature to allow [one] to take the Christian account seriously."[47] However, a careful reading of the Gospel accounts reveals no mythological origin. Perhaps you are familiar with stories of how Zeus fathered Hercules, Perseus, and Alexander, and of Apollo's fatherhood to Ion, Asclepius, Pythagoras, Plato, and Augustus. However, when we examine these stories we discover that "all the alleged parallels turn out to be quite different from the New Testament accounts. Almost all the pagan accounts involve a sexual encounter."[48] These myths "are nothing more than the stories about fornication between divine and human beings, which is something radically different from the biblical accounts of the virgin birth."[49]Jesus was not the result of sexual intercourse between God and Mary. Jesus is someone entirely set apart from ancient mythologies.

The Church and the Virgin Birth

The Early Church was unanimous in affirming the virgin birth as history. It is found in the Apostle's Creed, which reads "I believe . . . in Jesus Christ . . . who was conceived by the Holy Spirit, born of the Virgin Mary." The Nicene Creed of AD 325 affirms the virgin birth: "Who, for us men and for our salvation, came down from heaven, and was incarnate by the Holy Spirit of the Virgin Mary, and was made man." The fourth creed of the Early Church, the Chalcedonian Creed of AD 451, also bears witness that Jesus was "born of the Virgin Mary."

Because of its significance, the teaching of Christ's virgin birth is "*indispensable* to a biblically based Christology and Soteriology (the doctrine of salvation). Although we can imagine other ways by which God could supernaturally have kept Jesus sinless, in actuality the sign of the virgin birth is a historical nonnegotiable."[50] If our beliefs are to be governed by Scripture, then we cannot deny this teaching. Rejecting the virgin birth is rejecting the Word of God. Jesus is a miraculous gift to humanity and the world. He "is a gift that comes ultimately from God, but comes through Mary in a way that allows one to say that Jesus' origins are both human and divine."[51]

The Early Years of Jesus

Following his birth and the visit of the shepherds in the stable (Luke 2:8–20), Jesus was circumcised and then brought to the temple where he was honored by the prophecy of a man named Simeon and the testimony of a woman named Anna (Luke 2:21–38). Later he would be visited by the Magi (Matthew 2:1–12). The exact time is unclear. The wise men came to see him in a house, not a stable (Matthew 2:11), and Herod ruthlessly massacred "all the male children in and around Bethlehem who were two years old and under, in keeping with the time he had learned from the wise men" (Matthew 2:16). Joseph, being warned by an angel in a dream, fled Bethlehem before the murder of the baby boys, and he remained in Egypt until it was safe (Matthew 2:13–15). He then took Mary and Jesus to Nazareth, where Jesus would spend most of his life (Matthew 2:19–23; Luke 2:39–40).

The time from Jesus' early childhood to the beginning of his public ministry has rightly been referred to as "the silent years." The only record we have of any specific event is a trip to Jerusalem for the Passover when Jesus was about 12. He was left behind for several days and was eventually found astonishing the teachers at the temple with his knowledge (Luke 2:41–50). Only one particular statement made by Jesus is given, but it is significant. When asked by his mother why he had behaved in such an insensitive manner, causing his parents such anxiety (Luke 2:48), Jesus responded, "Didn't you know that I must be involved in my Father's interest?" (2:49). These words are the first of Jesus recorded in Scripture. Theologians often consider what is called Jesus' "Messianic consciousness." How and when did he know that he was God's Son, God's Christ, and the Savior of the world? Jesus' response to his parents points to the fact that already the things of God matter supremely to him. He must be involved in the work of divine things and therefore what better place for him to be than the temple.[52] Still more important is his phrase, "my Father's interest." The first words out of Jesus' mouth draw attention to the intimate relationship he enjoys with the Father. Darrell Bock says, "'My Father' suggests the mystery that is a part of Jesus' person. Jesus has a strong sense of identity with the Father and is committed to the mission God sent him to do."[53] Jesus is already aware of a close, filial relationship with the Father, and that he is here to do his will.

Luke provides a snapshot of "the silent years" in Luke 2:51–52. Jesus sets the example for all children in that he was obedient to his parents (2:51). He also grew or "increased" through the years "in wisdom and stature, and in favor with God and people" (2:52). His growth was normal and godly. We will not see him again, however, until his baptism by John the Baptist.

The Baptism of Jesus

This baptism event in the life of Jesus is recorded in all three of the Synoptic Gospels and it is also alluded to in John (Matthew 3:13–17; Mark 1:9–11; Luke 3:21–22; John 1:31–34). Jesus comes to John the Baptist, his cousin. John is hesitant to baptize Jesus. He realized that Jesus' life required no repentance or confession of sin. If anyone needed baptizing, it was John by Jesus (Matthew 3:13–14).[54] Jesus, however, admonished John that this baptism would "fulfill all righteousness" (Matthew 3:15). John relented and baptized Jesus, and a most remarkable thing happened. The heavens opened, and the Spirit of God descended upon Jesus like a dove. Then a voice from heaven said, "This is my beloved Son. I take delight in Him!" (Matthew 3:17). Why was he baptized? What does it mean that his baptism fulfilled all righteousness? Why does the Spirit descend upon him? What is the significance of the voice from heaven? I believe there are at least seven theological observations we can glean from all of this.

First, Jesus' baptism is the inauguration of his public ministry.

Second, his baptism identifies him with humanity.

Third, the baptism of Jesus was preeminently a public declaration of his submission to the will of the Father.

Fourth, the baptism of Christ is an occasion for a revelation of the Triune God.

Fifth, the baptism of Jesus was an opportunity for God the Father to honor his Son.

Sixth, the baptism of Jesus was when the Spirit of God anointed him for his public ministry.

Seventh, Jesus' baptism defined and set the course for the type of Messiah he would be.

Verse 17 is especially crucial. The Father's declaration is a combination of Psalm 2:7 and Isaiah 42:1. Psalm 2 is Davidic and Messianic. Isaiah 42 is the first of the Servant Songs. In the declaration of the Father, the course of ministry for Jesus is set. He is indeed the Messiah, but his Messiahship will be realized by suffering service. And his willingness to be this kind of Messiah, a Suffering Servant King, is immediately put to the test.

The Temptation of Jesus

This event is found in each of the Synoptic Gospels, with Matthew and Luke providing the most extensive accounts (Matthew 4:1–11; Mark 1:12–13; Luke 4:1–13). This testing of Jesus (the Greek verb "tempted" can also be rendered "tested"), was divinely intended. Note that it was the Spirit who led him into the wilderness.

Several important themes emerge from the temptation experience: 1) an underlying analogy between Moses and Jesus; 2) the striking analogy between the nation of Israel and Jesus in the wilderness; 3) the analogy between Adam and Jesus (the second Adam); 4) the crucial linkage of Matthew 3:13–17 and 4:1–11; and 5) the significance of the designation "Son" as a reference for Jesus.

The Devil (Greek *diabolos*) appears in Matthew 4:1, just after Jesus has been designated as God's Son in Matthew 3:17. The Devil shows up for the purpose of testing/trying him to see if there is reality to that claim. The Devil engages Jesus in three simple dialogues. Jesus has been fasting for 40 days. His only sustenance would have been water (Luke 4:2). He is hungry, starving no doubt, and the tempter appears in order to lure him into a trap. He issues three challenges, and the first two in Matthew are a direct attack upon the declaration from heaven of Jesus' Sonship.

"If you are the Son of God" (4:3, 6) is intended by the Devil to cause Jesus to consider just what the divine declaration means. "Since you are the Son of God" captures well the assumption of Satan. John Broadus points out that each of the temptations is a challenge to the Son's confidence in his Father. The first is a challenge to *under-confidence*: "Tell these stones to become bread" (4:3). The second is a challenge to *over-confidence*: "Throw yourself down from the pinnacle of the temple" (4:5–6). The third involved a challenge of *other-confidence*: "I will give you all these things [all the kingdoms of the world] if you will fall down and worship me" (4:8–9).[55]

It is instructive to see how Jesus responded. First, Jesus trusted the leading and the control of the Spirit, even as he is led into the wilderness. Second, to each of the temptations he responded with the Word of God. Three times Jesus says, "It is written." The implication is that the Word stands written for all time. Third, each quote comes from Deuteronomy against the background of Israel's wandering in the wilderness (Deuteronomy 8:3; 6:16; 6:13).

In the three confrontations, Jesus is steadfast in His devotion and submission to his Father's purpose and plan for his life, regardless of what that might entail. The third experience is especially significant. Jesus is challenged to give allegiance to Satan rather than his Father. Jesus steadfastly refuses, and Satan leaves ("for a time," Luke 4:13), and the angels come and serve him. This man is qualified to be Israel's Messiah. He will be the King who obtains his Kingdom by being the Suffering Servant of the Lord (Isaiah 53).

Could Jesus Have Sinned in His Incarnate State?

The issue of "impeccability" (Latin *non potuit pec-*

care, "not able to sin") or "peccability" (Latin *potuit non peccare* "able not to sin") of Christ has been debated by Christians for centuries. Two facts must be affirmed regardless of one's position:

1. Christ was genuinely tempted, and
2. Christ did not sin.

Those who hold to the peccability of Christ, that Christ could have sinned but did not sin, do so on the basis of texts like Hebrews 4:15: He "has been tested in every way as we are, yet without sin." If the temptation was genuine then Christ had to be able to sin. Otherwise, the temptation was not real. The strength of this view is that it honors the genuine humanity of Jesus, identifies our Lord with human persons, and holds that just as our temptations are real, his temptations were real. The weakness of this view is that it does not sufficiently consider Christ in his person as God. God cannot sin. Christ's deity and humanity cannot be separated or divorced from one another. He is now and forevermore the God-man.

Those who hold to impeccability believe Christ's temptations by Satan were genuine, but that it was impossible for Christ to sin. The purpose of the temptations was not to see if Christ could sin, but to demonstrate that he could not sin.

Christ has two natures, but he is one person. If the two natures could be separated, then he could sin in his humanity. However, the human and divine natures cannot be separated in the person of Christ. In the union of these two natures, the human nature submits to the divine nature (otherwise the finite is stronger than the infinite). Since the divine nature cannot sin, it is held that Christ could not have sinned.

The two things we started with are what we must hold on to with no compromise: 1) Jesus was genuinely tempted, and 2) Jesus did not sin. Scripture does not address directly the "could he have sinned?" question, and we should rest content in what has been revealed to us. Second Corinthians 5:21 and Hebrews 4:15 make clear that Jesus was sinless. I want to make this clear as well.

The Miracles of Jesus

One of the evidences in Scripture for the Messiahship and deity of Jesus are his miraculous works. The
Gospels record 35 separate miracles performed by
Christ. Matthew mentions 20; Mark records18; Luke
mentions20; and John builds his Gospel around 7
sign miracles. These signs, however, are not all of the
miracles performed by Jesus. Matthew, for instance,
alludes to 12 occasions when Jesus performed a number of miraculous works (4:23–24; 8:19; 9:35; 10:1, 8;
11:4–5, 20–24; 12:15; 14:14, 36; 15:30; 19:2; 21:14).
Each Gospel writer selected according to his purpose
from the large number of miracles Jesus performed.

Look at the Gospel of John. The first 11 chapters—
sometimes called "the book of signs,"—focus on 7
particular miracles performed by Jesus that point to
his deity and should cause us to put our faith in him
that we "may have life in his name" (John 20:31). In
fact, in John 20:30 the apostle specifically tells us, "Jesus performed many other signs in the presence of
his disciples that are not written in this book," and in

John 21:25, using hyperbole, John says, "And there are also many other things that Jesus did, which, if they were written one by one, I suppose not even the world itself could contain the books that would be written." John's 7 signs/miracles include:

1. Jesus turns water into wine. (2:1–11)
2. Jesus heals a nobleman's son. (4:46–54)
3. Jesus cures a paralytic. (5:1–16)
4. Jesus feeds 5,000 men. (6:1–15; the only miracle recorded in all four Gospels besides the resurrection)
5. Jesus walks on water. (6:16–21)
6. Jesus heals a blind man. (9:1–42)
7. Jesus raises Lazarus from the dead. (11:1–57).

Of course the greatest miracle of all occurs in John 20 with the raising of Jesus bodily from the dead.

The Transfiguration of Jesus

The transfiguration of Jesus is recorded in each

of the Synoptics (Matthew 17:1–8; Mark 9:2–13; Luke 9:28–36). Peter also alludes to the event in 2 Peter 1:16–18. Peter, James, and John accompany Jesus to a high mountain. Moses and Elijah appear, and our Lord is "transformed" (*HCSB*) or "transfigured" (*NIV*) before them. The word "suggests a change of inmost nature that may be outwardly visible or invisible."[56] This outward manifestation of the inward reality of Christ allowed the disciples "to glimpse something of his preincarnate glory (John 1:14; 17:5; Philippians 2:6–7) and anticipate his coming exaltation (2 Peter 1:16–18; Revelation 1:16)."[57] The heavenly declaration is also crucial. The language is reminiscent of our Savior's baptism (Matthew 3:13–17). God the Father again speaks and says, "This is my beloved Son. I take delight in him. Listen to him!" Moses and Elijah disappear from the scene with only Jesus remaining.

What is the Christological and theological significance of this miraculous event? First, the disciples receive a foretaste of Jesus' coming exaltation and kingdom. Second, it is a revelation of the glory and deity of the Son of God. Third, it is a confirmation of Peter's confession in Matthew 16:16: "You are the Messiah, the Son of the living God." Fourth, it is an encouragement in light of our Lord's prediction of his passion in Matthew 16:21. Fifth, it serves as a motivation for the task to which the disciples have been called. They must deny themselves, take up their cross and follow Jesus. The transfiguration says, "Look who you are following!" Sixth, it fulfills Matthew 16:28 which says, "I assure you: There are some of those standing here who will not taste death until they see the Son of Man coming in His Kingdom." The transfiguration gave them a vision of that kingdom. Seventh, it is a declaration of the Son's unique and definitive revelation of the Father to the world. Eighth, it is a witness to the Son's superiority to and fulfillment of the Law (Moses) and the Prophets (Elijah). Ninth, it is a reaffirmation of the Father's love and delight in his Son. Tenth, it is a restatement that Jesus is the Messiah (Psalm 2) who will realize his Kingdom as the Suffering Servant of the Lord (Isaiah 42).

Carson is correct when he says, "The narrative is clearly a major turning point in Jesus' self-disclosure . . . The contrast between what Jesus had just predicted would be his fate and this glorious sight would one day prompt Jesus' disciples to marvel at the self-humiliation that brought him to the cross and to glimpse a little of the height to which he had been raised by his vindicating resurrection and ascension."[58]

The Ascension of Jesus

The ascension of our Lord is recorded in the two volume work of Dr. Luke (Luke 24:50–53; Acts 1:9–11). It is also attested to and interpreted in several other weighty passages (e.g., John 14:12; Acts 2:33, 36; Ephesians 4:8, 10; Colossians 4:1; Hebrews 10:11-12; 1 Peter 3:22; 2 Peter 1:16-21). It is an aspect of our Lord's ministry which is neglected in many theologies. But there is significance in our Lord's ascension. It marks the conclusion of his earthly ministry and the initiation of his heavenly session.

What can we say about the significance of our Lord's ascension? First, it ended the earthly ministry of Christ. Second, it ended the period of his humiliation. His glory was no longer veiled (John 17:5; Acts 9:3, 5). Christ is now exalted and enthroned in heaven (Philippians 2:9–11). Third, it marks the entrance of resurrected humanity into heaven and the beginning of a new work in heaven (Hebrews 4:14–16; 6:20). Fourth, it made the descent of the Holy Spirit possible (John 16:7). Fifth, it is the necessary corollary of the resurrection. It is the abiding proof that the resurrection of Jesus was more than a temporary resuscitation. Sixth, it conveyed to the disciples that the appearances, which had occurred at intervals over a period of forty days, were at an end. Seventh, it suggested that Jesus was no longer to be perceived by physical sensation but by spiritual insight. Eighth, it provided the occasion for the commissioning for witness and the promise of the Spirit (Acts 1:1–8). Ninth, it provided for our Lord gifting his Church with gifted men (Ephesians 4:11). Tenth, it provided the occasion for the promise that he would come again (Acts 1:9–11).[59] The life of Jesus is a life like no other. He was born contrary to the laws of nature, reared in obscurity, lived in poverty, and only once crossed the border of the land in which he was born and lived, and then as a small child. He had no wealth or influence, neither training nor education in the world's schools. His relatives were inconspicuous and unimportant. His death was the height of shame and disgrace in his day. As a boy he puzzled erudite scholars. In manhood he ruled the course of nature, walked upon the waves, and healed multitudes. He never wrote a book, yet if everything he did were written in detail, the world itself could not contain the books that would be written. Throughout history great men have come and gone, yet he lives. Herod could not kill him, Satan could not seduce him, death could not destroy him, and the grave could not hold him. As King he is enthroned at God's right hand. As priest he has atoned for sin and now prays for us. As prophet he is the final spokesman for God. He is our ascended Lord and he has promised us he will come again!

CHAPTER 4

No Other Name/No Other Way

Jesus Christ, the Son of God, was born to die. Unlike any other person who has ever lived, he came into this world for the expressed purpose of dying as the perfect sacrifice for the sins of the world (1 John 2:2; 4:10). 1 John 4:14 teaches us, "The Father has sent the Son to be the Savior of the world." John Stott in *The Cross of Christ* reminds us, "Evangelical Christians believe that in and through Christ crucified God substituted himself for us and bore our sins, dying in our place the death we deserved to die, in order that we might be restored to his favor and adopted into his family."[60]

When we consider the death of Jesus, many questions naturally come to mind. Did Jesus have to die?

What did the death of Jesus accomplish? Is Jesus by virtue of his atoning death on the cross the only way to heaven? Is it true that there is no other name/no other way by which we can be saved (Acts 4:12)? It is to these very good questions we will turn our attention.

Why Did Jesus Die?

Two basic truths necessitated the death of Jesus: 1) the holiness and justice of God and 2) the sinfulness of man. Both truths are succinctly contained in Romans 3:23: "For all have sinned and fall short of the glory of God." Romans 3:26 is also crucial, for it says that by the substitutionary atonement of Jesus, God "demonstrated His righteousness at the present time, so that he would be righteous and declare righteous the one who has faith in Jesus."

The consequences of sin are many. Important among these consequences are the effects of sin upon our wills, the volitional element of men and women. Sin's entrance has brought about a sinful nature in all humanity, and each individual now acts according to his nature. Because of the entrance of sin into the world and our inheritance of Adam's sinful nature (Romans 5:12–19), we are by nature hostile to God and estranged from him (Romans 8:7; Ephesians 2:1–3). Spiritually we are dead to God. We are enemies of God (Colossians 1:21).

However, there is good news. God did not leave Adam and Eve and their descendants under the curse of judgment and death, but proclaimed to them in the *protoevangelium*—the promise of the seed of the woman who would restore to them what they had lost (Genesis 3:15; Galatians 4:4). This Conquering Seed has the image of God in the same sense that God had originally intended for Adam and Eve. Unlike the man and the woman, he uses the image for what was intended, namely, choosing the will of God and not the lies of the Evil One (Matthew 4:1–11; Philippians 2:6–11).

Fallen humanity participates in the restoration of the image of God in man through Christ by faith (2 Corinthians 5:17). Regeneration and the process of sanctification reverse the corruption of the image incurred at the Fall. Glorification will see its complete eradication. We look forward to a complete, perfect, redeemed and restored image through union with Christ. It is his cross that makes all of this possible.[61]

Was the Cross Necessary?

Theologians debate what is called the "ontological necessity" of the atonement. The question of the debate is significant: "Was Jesus' death on the cross the only way God could have saved us," or "Was it possible that he could have saved us some other way?" In other words, "Was the cross the 'most fitting way' but not the 'essential way' to save us?" I believe biblically and theologically it was necessary and essential. Paige Patterson states the biblical necessity well:

Is. 9:6   *Mt 4. 5:18*

> The Scriptures speak of the atonement as "necessary." Since the Scriptures prophesied such an event, the Scriptures of necessity had to be fulfilled. Remonstrat-

ing with Peter for his attempted intervention to save Jesus through a violent act, Jesus says,

> "Thinkest thou that I cannot now pray to my Father, and he shall presently give me more than twelve legions of angels? But how then shall the scriptures be fulfilled, that thus it must be?" (Matt. 26:53–54).

Again, Jesus left little doubt about his own perception of the nature and necessity of his mission when at Caesarea Philippi.

> "And he began to teach them, that the Son of man must suffer many things, and be rejected of the elders, and of the chief priests, and scribes, and be killed, and after three days rise again." (Mark 8:31).

> "He is not here, but is risen: remember how he spake unto you when he was yet in Galilee. Saying, The Son of man must be delivered into the hands of sinful men, and be crucified, and the third day rise again" (Luke 24:6–7).

One of the most interesting avowals of Jesus occurs in John 12:24 when the Lord appears to provide something of a rationale for the essential nature of the atonement, suggesting that unless a grain of wheat die it abides alone. Only if it dies does it bring forth fruit. To that striking affirmation can be added the lucid observation of the author of Hebrews who simply declares,

> "And almost all things are by the law purged with blood; and without shedding of blood is no remission" (Heb. 9:22).

What emerges thus far is that the atonement was in fact "necessary" in order to fulfill the Scriptures.[62]

However, there is a theological and personal consideration that is even more compelling in affirming the necessity of the sacrifice and death of the Son of God. Again Patterson gets to the heart of the issue:

> Add to these [Scriptural arguments] the intriguing scene in Gethsemane in which Jesus cries to his Father

for deliverance from the agony of making atonement. What kind of Father does it make of God if he insists that the Son endure the cross when there remained some other option available to the Father through which he could save men? If it be objected that this removes the atonement from being a free, loving act of God, we must reply that the necessity of a particular action in no way necessarily prevents the action from being free or loving. . . The point remains that God will have difficulty avoiding the charge of being a "cosmic sadist" if he failed to exercise other options to save men, while choosing instead to allow his beloved Son to be crucified.[63]

Stott and Patterson agree that the atoning sacrifice of Jesus was necessary, and that that necessity resided within the very nature and character of God himself. The offense of sin demands satisfaction, atonement, and that demand is found within God himself:

To say the he must 'satisfy himself' means that he must be himself and act according to the perfection of his nature or 'name.' The necessity of 'satisfaction' for God, therefore, is not found in anything outside himself but within himself, in his own immutable character. It is an inherent or intrinsic necessity. The law to which he must conform, which he must satisfy, is the law of his own being.[64]

The Son of God had to come. The Son of God had to die. God's holiness demanded satisfaction. God's love sent a Savior.

What Did the Cross Accomplish? – Theories of the Atonement

The work of Christ on the cross is a beautiful tapestry. Ideas like ransom, sacrifice, propitiation, reconciliation, justification and example are all present in Scripture. Like a tapestry, these ideas weave together to create a picture of the work of Christ. Throughout history different aspects of the atonement have been highlighted and emphasized. Sometimes the attention given helped clarify and enhance our understanding of what Jesus accomplished. Other times things got out of balance. A brief survey of the different theories that have been put forward is helpful. Then we will examine the biblical images found in Scripture. We will conclude our analysis with a defense of what we see as the foundational understanding of Christ's work: the doctrine of penal substitution.

1) The Recapitulation Theory. Irenaeus (AD 130–202) is the first to present a developed understanding of the death of Christ. Christ recapitulated in himself all the stages of human life, including those aspects that relate to us as sinners. The need for the atonement arises from the justice of God. Suffering is necessary because sin and guilt have come into the world, and divine justice cannot be satisfied except by penal punishment. Irenaeus saw men as enslaved by the powers of darkness, and redemption as freedom from these powers. The sacrifice of Christ in some sense is both penal and substitutionary. The means by which Christ broke the power of Satan is *recapitulation.* By going through the whole of human experience, Christ rendered a perfect obedience to God on behalf of humanity. He, in essence, reversed the course for mankind that Adam had set us on.

2) *Ransom To Satan (also called the "Classic" or "Dramatic") Theory.* The next major theory of the atonement was set forth by Origen (AD 185–254). The significance of Christ's death on the cross with the resurrection is victory over Satan and the demons. In some sense the death of Jesus is a ransom paid to the Devil for the claims he had on humanity. Through the Fall, Satan had obtained certain rights over us which Christ annuls by ransoming us. By an almost "holy deception," God defeated the Devil. Rufinus of Aquileia (c. AD 400) shows us how this view was understood: "The purpose of the Incarnation...was that the virtue of the Son of God might be as it were a hook hidden beneath the form of human flesh... to lure on the prince of this age to a contest; that the Son might offer him his flesh as a bait and that then the divinity which lay beneath might catch him fast with its hook."[65] This would be (wrongly in my judg-

ment) the dominate understanding of the atonement for almost 1,000 years, at least until the time of Anselm.

3) The Satisfaction Theory. This view was developed by Anselm of Canterbury (1033–1109) and would become extremely important in the Church's understanding of the atonement. Anselm's book, *Cur Deus Homo* (*Why God Became Man*) may be the most important book ever written on the atonement. The foundation for understanding the atonement is the awful debt of sin that falls upon man. Sin is an offense against God's honor and majesty, and it cannot go unpunished. Anselm rejected the ransom to Satan theory and contributed to its demise. Man is indebted to God, not to the Devil, and it is God's justice that demands satisfaction. Anselm argued that God could not simply forgive a debt without any satisfaction, and that man is incapable of rendering satisfaction to God. He reasoned that man must pay satisfaction, but that only God could provide satisfaction. God resolves the dilemma by means of the incarnation of the God-man, Jesus Christ.

4) The Moral Influence Theory. This view, popular among liberal theologians, was first articulated by Abelard (1079–1142). Abelard's view of the atonement rightly stresses the love of God, but misses the biblical balance of God's holiness. He saw nothing in the Divine Nature that requires satisfaction. God requires not justice but repentance. The work of Christ consists in providing an example of the love of God which inspires and awakens in us a reciprocal love. The life and sufferings of Christ were intended to break hard hearts whereby they are melted unto repentance, which then finds favor in the love of God. Christ's example moves us to love God, who in turn forgives us on the basis of that love. Berkhof is correct in his summary and assessment of this theory when he writes,

> This theory robs the atonement of its objective character, and thereby ceases to be a real theory of the atonement. It is at most only a one-sided theory of reconciliation. In fact, it is not even that, for subjective reconciliation is only possible on the basis of an objective

reconciliation. It really confounds God's method of saving man with man's experience of being saved, by making the atonement itself to consist in its effects in the life of the believer, in union with Christ.[66]

5) The Example ("Socinian") Theory. The Socinian movement began in the late sixteenth century through the teachings of Michael Servetus, but more particularly through Faustus and Laelius Socinius. All were Unitarians (i.e. they denied the Trinity) and rationalists. Christ's death did not atone for sin. By his teachings in life and his example in death, Christ brought salvation to man. Sin is not as serious as is commonly believed, and God, by an act of his will, may simply choose to forgive. Man's repentance (self-effort) causes God to will forgiveness and that is enough. The death of Christ is not a substitution but a "moral impetus." Christ gives us an example of how to love God and by his death he inspires us to do so.[67]

6) The Governmental Theory. Hugo Grotius (1583–1645) was a lawyer. His view of the atonement is similar to Socinianism. Christ suffered, not to pay for the sins of humankind nor to give us an example, but to show that, although God was willing to forgive, he still considered the transgression of his law a serious matter. God established the law (government of God) as merely a product or effect of his will. It is not something inward in God, therefore he has the power to alter it or abrogate it. God simply relaxes the claims of the law and saves sinners. However, to show his hatred of sin, he sends Christ who suffers and dies as an exhibition. There is no payment of debt, no one-for-one substitution, and no vicarious suffering. Sin disrupted God's government. By his death Christ demonstrated the high estimate God placed on his law and government. His law said, "The soul that sins shall die." Because God did not want sinners to die, he relaxed his law and accepted the death of Christ instead. Christ died as a public example of the depth of sin and the length to which God would go to uphold his moral law.[68]

7) *The Mystical Theory.* With the coming of the Enlightenment, rationalism and anti-supernaturalism, Christ was humanized and his work was radically

reevaluated. Christ's work in the post-Reformation period often departed from a penal satisfaction understanding of the atonement (Anselm and Calvin) to a moral influence or exemplary theory of the valiant, inspiring efforts of a good man to gain victory over the difficulties of life. Jesus was viewed more as a martyr than a Savior.

Friedrich Schleiermacher (1768–1834) said Christ suffered for our good and should fill us with love, with a "god-consciousness." Salvation does not lie in the cross of Christ but in his person. His nature is communicable (sharable) and salvation lies in this nature being imparted to us. The purpose of the incarnation is the deification of man. Jesus is the mirror of Divinity who awakens the Divine Consciousness within all who meet him. Christ's death simply exercises a positive influence to change man. Christ's unbroken unity with God enabled him to bring a potential mystical influence for good to humanity through his death.[69]

The Nature of the Atonement as Penal Substitution

Each of the theories just examined contain elements of truth—some more than others. However, when one carefully examines the whole of redemptive history and the crucial theological terms in Scripture, an inescapable conclusion is reached. The death of the Son of God on the cross accomplished a penal satisfaction or penal substitution for sinners. The Lord Jesus, by offering himself as a *sacrifice*, by *substituting* himself for us and actually bearing the punishment that should have been ours, *satisfied* the holiness, righteousness and justice of God and effected a *reconciliation* between God and man. Jesus took our place, bore our sin, became our curse, endured our penalty, and died our death.[70] This view is firmly rooted in the testimony of Scripture.

Christ's life and death certainly exemplified divine love and exerted an influence for good by providing a model of servanthood and sacrifice. I gladly affirm this truth. But more importantly, Christ's death provided for sinners a sinless substitutionary sacrifice that satisfies divine justice. He makes available to all an incomprehensibly valuable redemption delivering sinners from enslavement and reconciling and restoring sinners from estrangement to full fellowship and inheritance in the family of God. Several beautiful images in Scripture are employed to bring out the various components of his saving work.

The idea of "atonement" is the focal point of the Scriptural idea of the saving work of Christ (Isaiah 53:10; Romans 3:25; Hebrews 2:17; 1 John 2:2; 4:10). Christ's work on the cross satisfied the righteousness of God while effecting the same satisfaction regarding the guilt of sin. Atonement can only be rightly understood in light of the holiness and justice of God and the severity of the reaction of God's holiness to sin. God's holiness must be satisfied and the sins of humanity must be removed. Atonement is realized when God takes upon himself, in the person of Jesus, the sinfulness and guilt of humankind, so that his justice might be executed and the sins of men and women forgiven. It is essential to underscore this idea by affirming that God is moved to this self-sacrifice by his infinite mercy, love, and compassion.

The word "propitiation" (Greek: *hilaskomai*) is crucial and appears in four important texts: Romans 3:25, Hebrews 2:17, 1 John 2:2, and 1 John 4:10. To propitiate means to appease or satisfy. It is important to note that man is in no way involved in the act of propitiation. God satisfies himself through the sacrifice of his Son. God was in Christ reconciling the world to himself (2 Corinthians 5:18). J. I. Packer says it beautifully in his outstanding article, "What Did the Cross Achieve? The Logic of Penal Substitution":

> Christ's death had its effect first on God, who was hereby *propitiated* (or, better, who hereby propitiated himself), and only because it had this effect did it become an over-throwing of the powers of darkness and a revealing of God's seeking and saving love. The thought here is that by dying Christ offered to God *satisfaction* for sins, satisfaction that God's own character dictated as the only means whereby his 'no' to us could become a 'yes'. Whether this Godward satisfaction is understood as the homage of

death itself, or death as the perfecting of holy obedience, or an undergoing of the God-forsakenness of hell, which is God's final judgment on sin, or a perfect confession of man's sins combined with entry into their bitterness by sympathetic identification, or all these things together (and nothing stops us combining them together), the shape of this view remains the same—that by undergoing the cross Jesus expiated our sins, propitiated our Maker, turned God's 'no' to us into a 'yes', and so saved us.[71]

The idea of "redemption" is vitally related to the themes of liberation, deliverance and ransom. There is indeed a struggle between the Kingdom of God and the hostile, demonic powers enslaving humankind. Redemption is the idea of bringing sinners out of such hostile bondage into authentic freedom (Colossians 2:15). As redeemer, Jesus breaks the power of sin and sets sinners free. He creates a new and obedient heart by delivering us from the power of sin, guilt, death and Satan. He gathers a people who have been bought with a price, the precious blood of Christ (1 Peter 1:18–19).

"Redemption" is a metaphor from the world of commerce, war and slavery and finds its roots in the Exodus. The meaning of "to redeem" is normally to pay a ransom price for the release of a captive or a slave. Occasionally a word for purchase will stress just the opposite, saying that a free man has been purchased to be a slave of Christ. Central texts for redemption include Mark 10:45, Galatians 3:13, and 1 Timothy 2:6.

"Reconciliation" looks at the atonement through the picture of battle or broken relationships. It involves bringing fallen humanity out of alienation into a state of peace and harmony with God. Jesus, as reconciler, heals the separation and brokenness created by sin and restores communion between God and humankind. Reconciliation is not a process by which men and women become more acceptable to God, but an act by which we are delivered from estrangement to fellowship with God. Because of Christ's work on the cross, God has chosen to treat men and women in sin as his children rather than as sinners, enemies and transgressors (2 Corinthians

5:18–21; Ephesians 2:12–16; Colossians 1:20–22).

"Justification" looks at our relationship through the metaphor of law. Key texts include Romans 3:28; Galatians 2:16; 3:11. Romans 3:21-31 connects our justification to the propitiation or atonement of Jesus (Romans 3:25). God declares us justified in his sight, a standing of righteousness before him. To justify is to declare righteous. It is a judicial term indicating a verdict of acquittal. There is no longer any condemnation. The claims of God's law against the sinner have been fully satisfied. Justification is not an altering of God's righteous demands, for in Christ all of his demands have been fulfilled. Christ's perfect life of obedience to the law and his atoning death which paid sin's penalty are the bases for our justification (Romans 5:9).

Summarizing what Jesus accomplished on the cross, Packer makes nine observations:

1. God… 'condones nothing', but judges all sin as it deserves: which Scripture affirms, and my conscience confirms, to be right.

2. My sins merit ultimate penal suffering and rejection from God's presence (conscience also confirms this), and nothing I do can blot them out.

3. The penalty due to me for my sins, whatever it was, was paid for me by Jesus Christ, the Son of God, in his death on the cross.

4. Because this is so, I through faith in him am made 'the righteousness of God in him', i.e. I am justified; pardon, acceptance and sonship become mine.

5. Christ's death for me is my sole ground of hope before God. 'If he fulfilled not justice, I must; if he underwent not wrath, I must to eternity.'

6. My faith in Christ is God's own gift to me, given in virtue of Christ's death for me: i.e. the cross procured it.

7. Christ's death for me guarantees my preservation to glory.

8. Christ's death for me is the measure and pledge of the love of the Father and the Son to me.

9. Christ's death for me calls and constrains me to trust, to worship, to love and to serve.[72]

Charles Wesley would simply add, "Amazing love! How can it be, that Thou, my God, shouldst die for me!"

Other religions have a martyr, but Jesus' death was that of a Savior. It provides salvation from sins as Christ takes our place and dies our death. In this, his work on the cross was substitutionary. By his obedient life, he fulfilled the law for us and by his death on the cross, he satisfied the demands of the law for us. The cross of Christ is the actual execution of justice of God's unrelaxed penalty revealed in the law (Galatians 3:10–13). In Jesus, God's holy love is revealed; his holiness is completely satisfied and his love is clearly demonstrated (1 John 4:10). Hallelujah! What a Savior!

CHAPTER 5

THE RESURRECTION: FACT, FABLE OR FICTION?

Christianity stands or falls with the bodily resurrection of Jesus. The apostle Paul certainly understood it that way. In the great resurrection chapter of 1 Corinthians 15 Paul says, "If Christ has not been raised, then our preaching is without foundation, and so is your faith. In addition, we are found to be false witnesses about God, because we have testified about God that he raised up Christ – whom he did not raise up... And if Christ has not been raised, your faith is worthless; you are still in your sins" (15:14-15, 17).

It is difficult, if not impossible, to explain the birth of the Church and its gospel message apart from the resurrection of Jesus. The whole of New Testament faith and teaching orbits about the confession and conviction that the crucified Jesus is the Son of God established and vindicated by bodily resurrection (Romans 1:4). The doctrine of Jesus' bodily resurrection is no mere theoretical or esoteric discussion. William Lane Craig is correct when he notes the relevance of the resurrection now and for the future:

> Against the dark background of modern man's despair, the Christian proclamation of the resurrection is a bright light of hope. The earliest Christians saw Jesus' resurrection as both the vindication of his personal claims and as a harbinger of our own resurrection to eternal life. If Jesus rose from the dead, then his claims are vindicated and our Christian hope is sure; if Jesus did not rise, our faith is futile and we fall back into despair.[73]

It is not surprising that skeptics from outside the Church have attacked the bodily resurrection from the very beginning. However, it is disappointing when the attacks launched against the truth of Jesus' bodily resurrection are from those who claim to be a part of the Christian community, and there are many such persons today. Contemporary attacks on the bodily resurrection of Jesus are not new. They have existed since the period of the Enlightenment. As in the past, these current attacks simply attempt to mythologize the entire Christ event. But there is an answer to these attacks.

Resurrection Options

When one approaches the issue of the bodily resurrection of Jesus, those who affirm its truth bear the burden of proof. After all, we are making the claim that Jesus did what no other person has ever done. He died, rose from the dead and remains alive until this day. Adopting the model of historical investigation, we can quickly boil our options down to three.

First, we may say that the resurrection of Jesus is *false.* Jesus did not rise from the dead but certain persons, probably the disciples, fabricated a lie and pulled off one of the greatest hoaxes of all time.

Second, we may say that the resurrection of Jesus

is *fiction*, it is mythology. The Church over several decades made Jesus into someone and something he really was not. They began to tell stories about him that became more and more embellished over time.

Third, we may say that the resurrection is *fact*, and the supreme event of history. This view argues that the New Testament accurately records the historical and supernatural resurrection of Jesus of Nazareth from the dead. His resurrection was bodily and permanent. Further, the resurrected Christ was seen on numerous occasions by various witnesses who testified, some even to the point of martyrdom, to the reality of the resurrection. I hold to this view, but I will first examine some alternative theories.

Naturalistic Theories That Reject the Resurrection

Naturalistic theories attempt to explain away the idea that Jesus was bodily resurrected by God. Basically, advocates of this theory believe any naturalistic explanation of the event is better than a supernatural explanation. These theories were popularized by 19th century liberal theologians, and some of them are still advocated as we move into the early part of the 21st century.

1. The Swoon Theory – Jesus did not really die. He passed out as a result of enormous physical punishment. Later he revived and regained consciousness in the cool, damp tomb. Somehow he was able to unwrap himself from his grave clothes. He was also able to move the large stone that sealed the entrance to the tomb. Bruised, bleeding, battered and beaten, he emerged from the tomb and convinced his followers that he had risen from the dead.

2. The Spirit Theory – Jesus was not raised bodily, but returned in a spirit form. This view is sometimes popular with New Age mystics. Interestingly, this is also the view of Jehovah's Witnesses. They teach that Jesus was created by God as the archangel Michael and that while on earth he was only a man. Following his death on the cross God restored him in a spiritual form only. In *Let God Be True*, the Watchtower asserts,

"King Christ Jesus was put to death in the flesh and was resurrected an invisible spirit creature..."[74] In addition, "Jesus did not take his human body to heaven to be forever a man in heaven. Had he done so, that would have left him even lower than the angels... God did not purpose for Jesus to be humiliated thus forever by being a fleshly man forever. No, but after he had sacrificed his perfect manhood, God raised him to deathless life as a glorious spirit creature."[75]

3. The Hallucination Theory – David Strauss argued that "the imagination of his [Jesus] followers aroused in their deepest spirit, presented their master revived, for they could not possibly think of him as dead.... [It is to be] reduced completely to the state of mind and made into an inner event."[76] A modern version is that of Ian Wilson who believes Jesus pre-programmed his disciples to hallucinate by means of hypnosis.[77]

4. The Vision Theory – The disciples had experiences they interpreted to be appearances of the risen Jesus. They believed these to be literal and real appearances. Jürgen Moltmann believes that the dis-

ciples saw visionary appearances of the risen Christ
and that he communicated to them.[78]

5. The Legend/Myth Theory – Over time the Jesus stories were embellished and exaggerated. This
is basically the view of the *Jesus Seminar.* This view is
radically committed to an anti-supernatural agenda
that separates the Jesus of history (who he really was)
from the Christ of Faith (what the Church later imagined him to be). According to proponents of this theory, the resurrection is a wonder story indicating the
significance the mythical Jesus held for them.

6. The Stolen Body Theory – This is actually the
earliest theory that attempts to explain away the
bodily resurrection of Jesus. It goes back to Matthew 28:11-15, where it is recorded that the soldiers
who guarded Jesus' tomb were bribed by the Jewish
leaders to lie and say, "His disciples came during the
night and stole him while we were sleeping (28:13).
Some allege the body could also have been stolen by
the 1) Jewish leaders, 2) Romans, or even 3) Joseph
of Arimathea.

7. The Wrong Tomb Theory – Belief in the bodily

resurrection of Jesus rests on a simple mistake: first the women and later the men went to the wrong tomb. Finding it empty, they erroneously concluded that Jesus had risen from the dead. Craig informs us that this theory "was dead almost on arrival" when it showed up on the scene in the early 20th century.[79]

8. The Lie for Profit Theory – The alleged resurrection of Jesus was a "religious hoax." It was perpetuated by Jesus' disciples. His death by crucifixion was a huge disappointment, but his followers saw a way to turn it for good and financial profit. They began to proclaim that Jesus had risen, built a substantial following, and profited from the monies they were able to fleece from the people.

9. The Mistaken Identity Theory – This view says the women mistook someone who they thought was Jesus. They perhaps ran into a gardener or caretaker. It was dark, being early in the morning, and they could not see this man clearly. He may have been standing or working near an empty tomb, the wrong tomb. Informing them that Jesus was not there, they mistakenly believed he had risen.

10. The Twin Theory – This one is perhaps the most absurd of the naturalistic theories. Robert Greg Cavin argued that Jesus had an identical twin. They were separated at birth and did not see each other again until the crucifixion. Following Jesus' death, his twin conjured up a Messianic identity and mission for Jesus, stole his body and pretended to be the risen Jesus.[80]

11. The Muslim Theory – Islam rejects the biblical witness concerning the crucifixion of Jesus. God instead provided a substitute for Jesus, perhaps even making the person look like Jesus. Surah 4:157 in *The Koran* says, "They declared: 'We have put to death the Messiah Jesus the son of Mary, the apostle of Allah.' They did not kill him, nor did they crucify him, but they thought they did."[81] Among Muslims there is no unanimity on who took the place of Jesus. Candidates include Judas, Pilate, Simon of Cyrene or even one of the disciples.[82] Muslims do not believe in the bodily resurrection of Jesus because they do not believe he died.

Contemporary Models for Explaining the Resurrection

Gary Habermas has pointed out that the "Naturalistic Theories of the 19th Century" devoured each other so that they are seldom held today as they once were.[83] They were found to be flawed and scholars moved on. But where did they move to? After all, if you are committed to anti-supernaturalism from the start and you rule out in advance the possibility of the supernatural bodily resurrection of Jesus, what do you do? You develop more sophisticated theories that often turn out to be vague, fuzzy and unclear. Being cautious of oversimplification, we can summarize recent thinking on the bodily resurrection in terms of 5 models.

The first model is held by those who tend to either dismiss or at least seriously question the facticity of the resurrection appearances. These persons tend to dismiss any literal claims that Jesus' tomb was empty or that he was actually seen by his followers. They conclude that the nature of the original eyewitnesses' experiences cannot be discovered.

The second model is characterized by those more interested in the nature of the disciples' experiences and who may accept a literal resurrection of Jesus. However, these scholars still insist that these experiences cannot be historically verified. They can only be accepted by faith.

The third model is characterized by persons who believe the resurrection is probable, and who set forth a reconstruction of the historical nature of the appearances. They often provide reasons why the empty tomb is the best explanation for all of the data and they seek "to ascertain at least a minimalistic understanding of what really happened, including the providing of reasons for the acceptance of the appearances of Jesus and the empty tomb."[84] They still are convinced that the resurrection is not demonstrable by historical methodology. Jesus' appearances are usually viewed as spiritual in nature, rather than physical.

The fourth model believes available historical data is sufficient to demonstrate the probability that the tomb was empty and that Jesus was literally raised from the dead. The historical facts support the likelihood of the empty tomb and the literal appearances of Jesus.

The fifth model is the historic, orthodox position. Scholars here agree with the other groups that the evidence refutes the naturalistic theories. They further believe that the tomb in which Jesus was buried was found empty and that Jesus actually appeared to his followers. He rose from the dead in the same body in which he was crucified, though it was a transformed resurrection body (1 Corinthians 15).[85]

An Apologetic for the Bodily Resurrection of Jesus

Why should anyone believe in the bodily resurrection of Jesus? Is not the claim itself simply incredible from the start? After all we are making a one of a kind claim that has never been duplicated at any time, in any place, by any other person. Christians must, and do, bear the burden of proof on this, and the evidence must be both substantial and strong. Habermas is helpful at this point:

> Today, most critical theologians find much less history in the gospels than their 19th-century counterparts, to be sure. Yet, a substantial number of historical facts are recognized with regard to the death and resurrection of Jesus.

> Virtually all scholars today agree that Jesus died by crucifixion and that his body was afterwards buried. Due to his death, his disciples were despondent, believing that all hope was gone. At this point many contemporary scholars add that the burial tomb was found empty a few days later, but that it did not cause belief in the disciples.

> It is virtually unanimous that, soon afterwards, the disciples had experiences which they were convinced were appearances of the risen Jesus. These experiences transformed their lives as they believed that Jesus was literally alive. These experiences also emboldened

them to preach and witness in Jerusalem, the very city where Jesus had been crucified and buried only a short time previously. Here it was the message of Jesus' resurrection which was the central proclamation for these eyewitnesses.

History also relates that, due to this testimony, the Christian Church grew, featuring Sunday as the primary day of worship. Some scholars add here that one of the early Church leaders was James, the brother of Jesus, who was a skeptic until he believed he saw the risen Jesus. Basically all agree that a persecutor of the Church, Saul of Tarsus, was converted to Christianity by an experience which he also believed was an appearance of the risen Jesus.

These are a minimum number of facts agreed upon by almost all critical scholars who study this topic, whatever their school of thought. From this summary, at least eleven separate facts can be considered to be knowable history (while another is additionally recognized by many): (1) Jesus died due to crucifixion and (2) was buried afterwards. (3) Jesus' death caused the disciples to experience despair and lose hope, believing that their master was dead. (4) Although not as widely accepted, many scholars acknowledge several weighty arguments which indicate that the tomb in which Jesus was buried was discovered to be empty just a few days later.

Almost all critical scholars further agree that (5) the disciples had real experiences which they thought were literal appearances of the risen Jesus. Due to these experiences, (6) the disciples were transformed from timid and troubled doubters afraid to identify themselves with Jesus to bold preachers of his death and resurrection who were more than willing to die for their faith in him. (7) This message was the center of preaching in the earliest Church and (8) was especially proclaimed in Jerusalem, the same city where Jesus had recently died and had been buried.

As a direct result of this preaching (9) the Church was born, (10) featuring Sunday as the special day of worship. (11) James, a brother of Jesus who had been a skeptic, was converted when he believed that he saw the resurrected Jesus. (12) A few years later, Paul was also converted to the Christian faith by an experience which he, likewise, thought was an appearance of the risen Jesus.

Such facts are crucial in terms of our contemporary investigation of Jesus' resurrection. With the possible exception of the empty tomb, the great majority of critical scholars who study this subject agree that these are the minimal historical facts surrounding this event. As such, **any conclusions concerning the historicity of the resurrection should at least properly account for [all of] them.**

Now, it needs to be carefully noted that the actual resurrection of Jesus, in the sense of his exit from the tomb, is nowhere narrated in the New Testament. The teaching that he actually rose from the dead was a conclusion drawn from the fact that he had literally died, followed by his appearances in a transformed body to numerous individuals and groups.[86]

Having established these historical facts, which are widely agreed upon and accepted by those who study the resurrection of Jesus, we can proceed to build a case for the bodily resurrection of Jesus. Evidence for the resurrection of Jesus can be divided into two basic categories: 1) subjective evidence and 2) objective evidence. Subjective evidence is the evidence of experience. Here we ask the question, "Does an encounter with Jesus change lives? Do Christianity and Christ work? Perhaps no line of evidence is more powerful than this when it comes to sharing your faith. Telling others who you were before you met Jesus, how you received him as Savior and Lord, and the difference he has made in your life is a powerful witnessing tool.

However, we must recognize and acknowledge that other religions claim to have religious experiences. Buddhists, Hindus, Muslims, Jews, New Agers and others often proclaim to have had an experience that changed their lives. Experience in and of itself is not sufficient to make the case. Therefore, we also need objective evidence, historical and verifiable. Here is the question we want to answer: Does the evidence *persuade* us that we have good reason for believing this alleged event really happened? We can indeed marshal a strong case of compelling evidence that Christ did rise from the dead. Observe the following evidence:

1. The birth of faith in the disciples and the radical change in their lives. J. P. Moreland says this about the disciples:

> They were willing to spend the rest of their lives proclaiming this [the resurrection of Jesus], without any payoff from a human point of view. It's not as though there were a mansion awaiting them on the Mediterranean. They faced a life of hardship. They often went without food, slept exposed to the elements, were ridiculed, beaten, imprisoned. And finally, most of them were executed in torturous ways. For what? For good intentions? No, because they were convinced beyond a shadow of a doubt that they had seen Jesus Christ alive from the dead. What you can't explain is how this particular group of men came up with this particular belief

without having had an experience of the resurrected Christ. There's no other adequate explanation.[87]

According to the traditions of the Church, each of the disciples, with the possible exception of John, died the death of a martyr. Each of them died alone, and yet each of them died proclaiming Jesus as the risen Lord. The importance of this can scarcely be overstated. While it is the case that persons will die for a lie, they will not die for what they know is a lie. It is highly unlikely that all of the disciples would die in this way if they concocted the resurrection story.

2. The empty tomb and the discarded grave clothes. The Christian movement could have been quickly crushed and put out of commission by one act: producing the corpse of Jesus. Evidently, based on the evidence, no one was able to do this.

3. Women were the first to testify. In the Jewish culture of the 1st century women were not qualified to be witnesses in a legal proceeding. They were deemed unreliable and therefore they could not testify in a court of law. Given this fact, it is amazing that the

Bible records that women saw the risen Jesus first. If the Early Church was trying to persuade people to believe Jesus rose from the dead, saying that women saw him first was not a wise strategy. The only reason to say women saw him first is because women saw him first.[88]

4. *Change in the day of worship from the Sabbath to Sunday by Jews.* Jewish identity is connected to their observance of the Sabbath. Yet something happened around AD 30 that caused a large group of Jews in Jerusalem to change their day of worship from the Sabbath to Sunday. Whatever happened would have to have been extraordinary.

5. *Unlikely nature of mass hallucination.* It's quite a leap of faith to believe all involved hallucinated together about the resurrection event.

6. *Numerous and varied resurrection appearances which lasted for 40 days and then abruptly ended.* These records corroborate each other. Ten distinct appearances stand out and are worth listing:

Appearances	Witnesses
1. John 20: 11-18	Mary Magdalene
2. Matthew 28:1-10	Other women
3. Luke 24:34, 1 Corinthians 15:5	Peter
4. Luke 24:13-15	Two disciples on Emmaus Road
5. Luke 24:36-43, John 20:19-25	Ten apostles
6. John 20:26-31, 1 Corinthians 15:5	Eleven apostles
7. John 21:1-22	Several apostles
8. Mathew 28:16-20, 1 Corinthians 15:6	The apostles and more than 500 disciples
9. 1 Corinthians 15:7	James, Jesus' half-brother
10. Luke 24:44-52, Acts 1:4-9	The disciples at his ascension

7. The 50 day interval between the resurrection and the proclamation of the gospel at Pentecost (Acts 2) in Jerusalem. What would explain the delay in public witness which could only hurt their cause? The biblical witness is clear. They waited until Jesus had ascended (Luke 24; Acts 1) and the Holy Spirit had come to empower them for witness (Acts 2). Christ had to leave before they would act on their own, and the Spirit had to come to give them boldness for witness.

8. Neither the Jewish leaders nor the Romans could

disprove the message of the empty tomb. All they had to do was produce the body of Jesus and the Christian movement was dead. It appears there was no body to produce.

9. The unexpected nature of the bodily resurrection of Jesus. The disciples did not anticipate that Jesus would rise from the dead, though he had predicted it on several occasions (Mark 8:31-33; 9:30-32; 10:32-34). In fact Mark 9:32 tells us they did not understand. Perhaps they thought he was again speaking in parables. When Jesus was crucified their hopes were dashed. They looked for and hoped for a mighty Messiah who would restore the glory of Israel as in the days of King David. A dying and rising Messiah was not what they expected, in spite of the fact the Old Testament predicted him.

10. The conversion of 2 skeptics: James the half-brother of Jesus and Saul of Tarsus. It's unlikely Jesus' little brother—who originally did not believe—would come around and believe after the resurrection unless it was true. It's also unlikely that a religious zealot, a murderer of Christians, would become one of them unless something radical happened.

11. The moral character of the eyewitnesses. The New Testament provides the greatest teachings found in any literature on love, truth, honesty, hope, faithfulness, kindness, and the list goes on. These teachings come from the pens of men like Matthew, John, Paul, James, and Peter. To affirm their teachings and yet reject their witness to Jesus as a lie or mistake is nonsensical. If we cannot or will not trust their testimony about Jesus, it is not wise to trust them concerning how to live life.

12. The early creedal witness of 1 Corinthians 15:3-7. The resurrection was the heart of the earliest Christian teaching. This is based on 1 Corinthians 15:3-7, where virtually all scholars agree that Paul recorded a very early creed concerning Jesus' death and resurrection. Some even date Paul's reception of this creed within a decade of the crucifixion itself (AD 30-40). Paul probably received this material during his visit in Jerusalem with Peter and James, who are included in the list of resurrection appearances (1 Corinthians 15:5, 7; Galatians 1:18-19).

13. The accepted character and claims of Jesus. Jesus on numerous occasions spoke of his crucifixion and resurrection. He claimed he was God (John 8:58; 10:30; 14:9), and he said he would come back from the dead (Matthew 16:21). To claim Jesus as a great religious figure and moral teacher and yet believe he got it wrong on his prediction of his resurrection will not work. If the resurrection is not true, then he was either a liar or a lunatic.

14. Reliable eyewitness documents recording the events. The New Testament is the most well authenticated document of antiquity. No textual critic of any theological persuasion would deny this.[89]

The Theological Significance of the Resurrection of Jesus

The resurrection is crucial for Christian theology. It ensures the truthfulness of doctrines such as the deity of Jesus Christ (Acts 2:22-24; Romans 1:3-4), the gospel (Acts 17:30-31), heaven (1 Peter 1:3-5), and hope for the believer's resurrection (1 Corinthians 15).[90] The resurrection indicates God's approval of Jesus. This includes his message concerning how one receives eternal life (John 14:6). The resurrection is unlike any other miracle. Jesus' resurrection was the very manifestation of eternal life. Jesus is now immortal; he will never die again. When the disciples witnessed the resurrection appearances of Jesus, they were actually confronted with living, walking, talking, eternal life. Jesus affirms this existence is a reality for all of his followers.[91]

First Corinthians 15, in particular, emphasizes the importance and nature of Christ's resurrection and its significance for the believer. The validity of the Christian faith rests upon it (15:12-19). It is integral to the gospel (15:1-11), our future hope (15:20-28), and Christian ethics (15:29-34). The bodily resurrection of Christian believers is consistent with natural principles of transformation and variation within kinds (15:35-49). Hence, we like Christ can be resurrected and not lose our identity. Since the salvation, motivation, and anticipation of the believer are based upon it, the resurrection is one of the few doctrines which cannot be overemphasized. It must have significant priority. It is the foundation of steadfastness and fruitfulness in the work of the Lord, because the laborer can have assurance that his labor is not in vain (15:58).

The hope of the Gospel also is eschatological in nature (Luke 24:45-48; Acts 2:27, 35; 1 Corinthians 15) and the resurrection is at the core of the Christian gospel and Christian theology. It tells us that the God who raised Jesus from the dead exists. It establishes Jesus' lordship. It establishes the doctrine of justification, which was accomplished on the cross and vindicated by Jesus' resurrection. The resurrection promises victory over death (John 14:1-9; 1 Corinthians 15:55-57), and the resurrection is a pledge of God's final judgment (Acts 17:31; Hebrews 9:26-27).

I do not always agree with the theology of the German theologian Karl Barth. However, when it comes to the significance of the relationship between the cross and the resurrection I believe he is correct:

The Resurrection: Fact, Fable or Fiction?

The mystery of the incarnation unfolds into the mystery of Good Friday and of Easter. And once more it is as it has been so often in this whole mystery of faith, that we must always see two things together, we must always understand one by the other … for there is no *theologia cruces* which does not have its complement in the *theologia gloriae*. Of course, there is no Easter without Good Friday, but equally certainly there is no Good Friday without Easter![92]

CHAPTER 6

WHO DO YOU SAY THAT I AM?

What has the Church believed about Jesus? What do some current thinkers believe? The question "Who is Jesus" is a question every generation must face and answer.

The Witness of History to Jesus of Nazareth

The Church has always believed certain basic tenets concerning the person and work of Jesus Christ. Bernard Ramm says there is a definitive view of Jesus that has been believed by Greek Orthodox, Roman Catholics, and evangelical Protestants until this day. Those non-negotiable tenets include the following:

1. There is a true incarnation of the *Logos*, the second person of the Triune God. The Son of God actually and truly assumed the whole of human nature.

2. There is a necessary distinction between the natures of Jesus Christ and his person. He is a single person who possesses the totality of both the divine and human natures.

3. The God-man is the result of the incarnation. Jesus Christ is not a double being, a compound being or some kind of hybrid being. He is the one Person of our Lord Jesus Christ, complete in his deity and perfect in his humanity.

4. In the incarnation there is no qualification or diminution of either Christ's deity or his humanity. Each nature retains its own integrity and genuineness.

5. There is a genuine hypostatic union in which the divine nature and the human nature come together and are present in the one person Jesus Christ. This union is real, supernatural, personal, inseparable, and permanent. There is today in heaven a God-man.

6. The whole of Christ's work, that is all that he does,

is to be attributed to his person and not to one or the other nature exclusively.

7. Jesus Christ exists only by means of the incarnation. There is no Jesus of Nazareth who possesses an independent life of his own. There was a time when Jesus did not exist. There has *never* been a time when the Son did not exist.[93]

The first 500 years of Church history was a time when the Church was especially active in wrestling with how to understand and comprehend the biblical portrait of Jesus. Two issues stand out in particular: the monotheism that Christianity inherited from Judaism and the fact that the New Testament clearly affirmed Jesus as God. How could these competing truths be reconciled?

The Road to the Christological Councils

The Church was forced to confront the issue of Christ's deity and its monotheistic faith early in its history. We find evidence of the struggle even in the New Testament. First John was written, in part, to confront a heresy known as *docetism*. False teachers did not confess Jesus of Nazareth as the Christ (1 John 2:22) and denied the Son had come in the flesh (1 John 4:2-3; 2 John 7). It is likely these false teachers were influenced by early Gnostic ideas. Gnosticism was a heretical movement that flourished in the 2ⁿᵈ century. The word *gnosis* in Greek means knowledge. Though Gnosticism developed into many forms, two basic teachings were: 1) salvation comes by mystical knowledge, and 2) matter is inferior or evil.

John battled the Docetists, as well as a man named Cerinthius. Docetism comes from the Greek word *dokeo,* which means "to seem" or "to appear." Docetists denied the reality of the incarnation. Jesus only appeared to have a body. Since matter was evil, the true God could have nothing to do with the creation of this material world (that was accomplished by an inferior power, the "Demiurge"). However, he sent the Christ to rescue our souls. This Christ cannot be incarnate however, for this would involve his taking to himself sinful and evil flesh (matter). Christ only appeared to have a body (Docetism), something John refutes in John 1:1, 14, 18 and 1 John 1:1-4, or the Christ temporarily adopted the man Jesus (Cerinthianism). In this view "the Christ" came upon the man Jesus at his baptism (Matthew 3:13-17) but left him prior to his death on the cross (Matthew 27:46). John refutes this heresy in 1 John 5:6-8.[94] The Church Father Ignatius (d. ca. AD 110) countered the Docetists in his letter to the Ephesians when he writes,

> For there are some who maliciously and deceitfully are accustomed to carrying about the Name while doing other things unworthy of God. You must avoid them as wild beasts. For they are mad dogs that bite by stealth; you must be on your guard against them, for their bite is hard to heal. There is only one physician, who is both flesh and spirit, born and unborn, God in man, true life in death, both from Mary and from God, first subject to suffering and then beyond it, Jesus Christ our Lord.[95]

And again in his letter to the Trallians he charges,

Be deaf, therefore, whenever anyone speaks to you apart from Jesus Christ, who was of the family of David, who was the son of Mary; who really was born, who both ate and drank; who really was persecuted under Pontius Pilate, who really was crucified and died... who, moreover, really was raised from the dead... But if, as some atheists (that is, unbelievers) say, he suffered in appearance only (while they exist in appearance only!), why am I in chains? And why do I want to fight with wild beasts? If that is the case, I die for no reason; what is more, I am telling lies about the Lord.[96]

In similar fashion the Church Father Irenaeus (c. 130 – c. 200) rejected the Cerinthians. In *Against Heresies (Refutation and Overthrow of the Gnosis Falsely So Called)* he exposes the error of the Gnostics, including those of Cerinthius:

John, the disciple of the Lord, proclaimed this faith and wished by the proclamation of the gospel to destroy the error which had been planted among men by Cerinthius...Now according to them neither was the

Word made flesh, nor Christ, nor the Savior... For they allege that the Word and Christ never came into this world, and that the Savior was neither incarnate nor suffered, but that he descended as a dove upon that Jesus ... and when he had proclaimed the unknown Father, ascended again...[97]

Ebionism was another early heresy that rejected the reality of the incarnation and the deity of Jesus. An offshoot of the Judaizers and committed to asceticism, they denied the essential deity of Jesus. Jesus was the prophet predicted by Moses in Deuteronomy 18:15, but he was not the preexistent Son of God. Jesus was made the anointed one at his baptism, a form of adoptionism similar to Cerinthianism, and he was chosen because of his perfect obedience to the law, something highly esteemed by the Ebionites.[98] Irenaeus also addressed this teaching: "Vain also are the Ebionites who do not accept in their souls by faith the union of God and man... not wishing to understand that the Holy Spirit came upon Mary, and the power of the Most High overshadowed her, and so what was born [of her] is holy and the Son of God Most High..."[99]

Debate and discussion concerning the person of Christ, his nature, and his relationship to the Father would continue into the 2nd and 3rd centuries, eventually leading to the four great Christological councils:

325 Nicea

381 Constantinople

431 Ephesus

451 Chalcedon

Prior to these four councils, Origen (c. 185 – c. 254) argued for the eternal generation of the Son, but also for his essential subordination.[100] Essential subordination teaches that the Son is truly subordinate to the Father in his essence, being, and person. The dynamic monarchianism or adoptionists such as Theodotus of Byzantium and Paul of Samosata (c. AD 260) continued to argue that God adopted Jesus as a unique and special man on whom his power would rest. Again, there was a denial of his full deity and eternality. This heresy would undergo some modification with men named Lucian and Arius, and it would provide the catalyst for the Nicene Council. Arianism, as we will see, is the forerunner of the modern Jehovah's Witnesses.

There were, on the other hand, those who wanted to maintain radical monotheism and yet affirm the deity of Jesus Christ. They have come down to us in history by the designations of modalistic monarchianism, patripassionism, or Sabellianism (named after a major proponent). This false teaching affirms that the three persons of the deity are simply three ways (or "modes") in which the one God has revealed or manifested himself. Father, Son, and Holy Spirit are in a sense simply names. They do not constitute genuine and real distinctions. The Father is the Son is the Holy Spirit is the Father. It could be said that the Father was born at Bethlehem and crucified at Calvary (hence the term "patripassionism" meaning "the suffering of the Father"), but at the time he was manifest as the Son and was called Jesus. The Church Father Tertullian (c. 155 – 220) wrote a major work against a prominent supporter of this view. In *Against Praxeas* he writes,

> In various ways has the Devil rivaled and resisted the truth. Sometimes his aim has been to destroy the truth by defending it. He maintains that there is only one Lord, the Almighty Creator of the world, in order that out of this *doctrine of the* unity he may fabricate a heresy. He says that the Father himself came down into the Virgin, was himself born of her, himself suffered, indeed, was himself Jesus Christ.[101]

So while controversy riddled the Early Church over phrases and concepts such as "*trinity,*" "unity of *substance,*" and "three *persons,*" the implications of these terms would only be worked out in the first four Councils of the Church.

The Council of Nicea (AD 325)

The Roman emperor Constantine convened the Council of Nicea because a major theological dispute between Alexander, bishop of Alexandria, (d. 328) and one of his presbyters, Arius (c. 250-336), became problematic and threatened the unity of the empire. Arius had adopted the theology of Paul of Samosota, who taught a form of adoptionism or dynamic monarchianism. This teaching emphasized the manhood of Jesus, but did so at the cost of his deity. When Paul of Samosata thought of "the Word" being in Jesus, it only meant the impersonal power of God. Jesus was a man who was controlled by "the Word," the power of God. Arius, following his teacher Lucian, built on this perspective. He viewed Jesus as less than fully God. There is only one true God who is eternal, immutable and indivisible. The Christ must be of a different substance. God must have created Christ, a creature that has a beginning. Being created, his essence is substantially different from God's, yet he is created out of nothing. The Arian party had two main points of contention going into the council of Nicea: Jesus is not coeternal, and he is created from nothing.

Arius was opposed by Alexander, and his young

protégé, the famous Athanasius (c. 296 – 373), so when the leaders of the Church convened in AD 325, supporters of both Arius and Alexander were present. However, the largest group at the council was the "middle of the road" contingency whose main spokesman was the Church historian, Eusebius of Caesarea (c. 265 – 339). Many in this group had orthodox instincts, but little biblical understanding of why they believed what they believed.[102] On May 20 the council began. There were approximately 318 bishops in attendance. Debate would center on the key term *homoousia*, which affirmed that the Son was fully divine and of the same substance/essence as the Father. Alexander and his followers were successful, and the result of the first Church Council is what we know as the Nicene Creed.

The Nicene Creed:

"We believe in one God, the Father All Governing, Creator of all things visible and invisible;

And in one Lord Jesus Christ, the Son of God, begotten of the Father as only begotten, that is, from the essence of the Father, God from God, Light from Light, true God from true God, begotten not created, **of the same essence [homoousion]** as the Father, through whom all things came into being, both in heaven and earth; Who for us men and for our salvation came down and was incarnate, becoming human. He suffered and the third day he rose, and ascended into the heavens. And he will come to judge both the living and the dead....

But, **those who say**, Once he was not, or he was not before his generation, or he came to be out of nothing, or who assert **that he, the Son of God, is of a different hypostasis or ousia**, or that he is a creature, or changeable, or mutable, **the Catholic and Apostolic Church anathematizes them**." [emphasis mine]

The Council of Constantinople (AD 381)

This council was called by Emperor Theodosius. It put to an end Arianism, which had experienced several resurgences in the 50 years following Nicea. It reaffirmed the decision of the Council of Nicea and completed the final version of the Nicene Creed. It also condemned the teachings of a man named Apollinarius (c. 310-390). If Arius erred by denying the deity of the Son, Apollinarius erred by overemphasizing it.

Apollinarius was a staunch defender of the Nicene doctrine and a friend of Athanasius. He taught that while all other human beings are body, soul, and spirit coexisting in a union (trichotomy), in Christ there was only the human body and soul. The divine *Logos* displaced the human spirit (*nous*). Christ was perfect God, but he lacked a complete humanity. Apollinarius held to a very literal interpretation of John 1:14 – Jesus took on a human body *alone*, not the human spirit. Jesus, then, did not have a human will, but only a divine will. Jesus had a human body and a divine spirit. The *problem* is that the divine swallows up the human. This view essentially denies the full humanity of Jesus Christ. It is not only our human bodies that need redemption; it is also our soul and spirit, our inner person that needs saving as well. Christ had to be fully and truly man if he was to save the whole of us. As Gregory of Nazianzus argued, "For that which he has not assumed he has not healed; but that which is united to his Godhead is also saved."[103] Constantinople affirmed the full humanity of the Son.

The Council of Ephesus (AD 431)

This council saw the condemnation of a man named Nestorious (d. AD 451). Nestorianism is the view that there are *two separate persons* in Christ: a human person and a divine person. Within a single body resides two persons. This view was rejected because nowhere in Scripture do we see the human nature of Christ acting as an independent person, deciding to do something contrary to the divine nature of Christ. Rather, we have a consistent picture of a *single* person always acting in wholeness and unity. The council insisted that Jesus was one person, although possessing both a human nature and a divine nature.

The Council of Chalcedon (AD 451)

This is the final and climatic of the four Christological Councils. In many ways it solidifies and establishes what the Church believes the Bible teaches concerning the person of Christ. It incorporates the major components of the three previous Councils. Its affirmations concerning Christ will not be attacked until the time of the Enlightenment when rejection of supernaturalism will call for a redefining of the person and work of Christ.

A man by the name of Eutyches (ca. 378 – 454) was condemned, excommunicated, and deposed. He held a view called monophysitism, meaning "one nature." Eutyches taught that the human nature of Christ was taken up and absorbed into the divine nature, so that both natures were changed, and thus a new 3rd kind of nature resulted. Jesus, according to this view, was a mixture of divine and human elements in which both were somewhat modified to form one new nature. The problem here is that Christ is neither truly God nor truly man. If that is so, then he could not truly represent us as a human being nor could he be true God and thus be able to pay sin's penalty and redeem us as our substitute. The 630 bishops gathered and formulated the Chalcedonian Creed, which sought to summarize and address the problems that had plagued the Church with regard to the person of Christ. It argued against:

1. *Docetism*: the Lord Jesus was perfect in his humanity and truly human, consubstantial with us according to his humanity and born of the Virgin Mary.

2. *Adoptionism*: it argued for the eternality of the *Logos* "begotten of the Father before the ages." He has always existed as God the Son.

3. *Modalism*: it distinguished the Son from the Father both by the titles of "Father" and "Son" and by the reference to the Father having begotten the Son before time began. The Father is not the Son.

4. *Arianism*: it affirmed that the Lord Jesus was perfect in his deity, truly God.

5. *Apollinarianism*: it confessed that the Lord Jesus Christ was "truly man of a reasonable soul [spirit]

and body...consubstantial with us according to his humanity; in all things like unto us."

6. *Nestorianism*: it affirmed Jesus' full deity and the truth of a real incarnation. It also spoke throughout of *one* and the *same* Son and *one* person and *one* subsistence, not parted or divided into two persons and whose natures are *in union* without division and without separation.

7. *Eutychianism*: it confessed that in Christ there were *two* natures without confusion and without change, the property of each nature being preserved and concurring in the one person.

Chalcedon argues that Christ is "one person with two natures," with that person being the Son of the Triune God. The eternal Son of God took to himself a truly human nature, and Christ's divine and human natures remain distinct and retain their own properties. Yet, they are inseparably united together in one person. In other words, Jesus Christ is fully God and fully man. Taking on a human nature did not involve mixing divine attributes with human nor converting one nature to the other. The two natures are inseparably joined together in one person now and forever.

Nicene-Chalcedonian Christology affirms that in our Lord Jesus Christ we come face to face with God. We meet God not subsumed under human flesh, not merely associated with it, not merely accompanying it, not merely shining through it, but in undiminished moral splendor, giving to humanity the moral completeness which has been missing since the time of the fall. In Christ we see all that Adam was intended to be, but never was, all that we are not but which we will become through resurrection and glorification (1 John 3:1-3).[104]

Christology in the Church Councils

The Resolution of Trinitarian Relationships and the Hypostatic Union of Christ

Error Against Deity	Church Position	Errors Against Humanity
Arius Christ is a Created Being	Nicea, 325 Christ is eternal and truly God	
	Constantinople, 381 Full humanity of Christ is affirmed	Apollinarius dominant logos over the humanity
Nestorius Christ is two natures in a mechanical union	Ephesus, 431 Unity of Christ's personality is confirmed	
	Chalcedon, 451 Orthodox Christology Established: Two natures in one person	Eutyches divine nature shallows up the human nature

Modern Attacks on the Christ of the Bible

As we move forward in the early 21st century, the Christ we find in the Bible—the Christ confessed by the Church for most of its history—is not acceptable to many. Attacks come from several directions, yet virtually every attack is comprised of two common characteristics: 1) a denial of Christ's deity, and 2) a rejection of his work on the cross as the sufficient provision for salvation.

The Jesus of liberalism is an outgrowth of what has been called "the quest for the historical Jesus."[105] This designation caught on as a result of the landmark work by Albert Schweitzer, *The Quest for the Historical Jesus* (1906). Frederick Schleiermacher (1768 – 1834) was the most influential theologian of the 19th century and has rightly been called the father of modern liberal theology. He helped launch the attacks on the Jesus of the Bible. Schleiermacher offered an adoptionist understanding of Jesus that rejected his preexistence. Jesus was not the eternal Son of God become human, the *Logos* incarnate. For

Schleiermacher, what distinguished Jesus from other humans was "the constant potency of his God-consciousness, which was a veritable existence of God in him."[106] He presented Jesus as a God-filled man, not the God-man. This Jesus, who differed from us only in degree, not kind, is an inspiring example for us to follow. He is not our Savior in the biblical understanding.

At a later date (c. 1880-1920) the history-of-religions school would come to dominate. It argued that Christ's preexistence and incarnation were only myths intended to give him a stature equal to that of other heroic figures of antiquity. A distinction was created between the *Jesus of history* (the man who actually lived) and the *Christ of Faith* (the mythical Christ created in the minds of the Early Church). It is out of this boiling cauldron of redefining Christ that the "Quest for the Historical Jesus" emerged, a quest that is still active today.

The quest for the historical Jesus, with its post-Enlightenment skepticism, anti-supernatural bias, and goal of rigorous scientific methodology, began in earnest in the latter part of the 19th century. While this movement was not monolithic, these scholars assumed the Bible's basic untrustworthiness regarding the person of Jesus. This skepticism manifested itself most clearly in the Jesus Seminar that appeared in the mid-eighties and emerged full-fledged with its publication of *The Five Gospels* in 1993. The Seminar came together to determine what Jesus actually said and did. They rated his sayings in Matthew, Mark, Luke, John, and the non-biblical Gospel of Thomas according to a color code. The Seminar argued that 82% of the words attributed to Jesus do not come from him. Jesus, they said, was not interested in eschatology or judgment. He was basically a teacher who used funny sayings and parables. Much of what we find in the Gospels is the Early Church's work. There is not much that really goes back to Jesus.

What should be our response to all this? I believe there are a number of shortcomings in the methods and conclusions of liberal Christologies. I will quickly note 10.

1. Their anti-supernatural worldview biases their evaluation of the biblical material from the start. They are not really open to where the data might lead because they have determined in advance where it must lead: to a purely human Jesus who cannot be God.

2. All the information we have on Jesus demands that he look like a 1st century Jew who spent his life in Israel. That is who he was. The New Testament agrees.

3. The object of Christian Faith is the Triune God revealed in history and the Old and New Testaments. Here we discover the promise of a Savior (OT) and the coming of that Savior (NT). The flow of redemptive history is something all the liberal Christologies fail to appreciate.

4. The Jesus of history and the Christ of faith cannot be separated, for they are one and the same. Therefore it is not surprising that each quest, including the Jesus Seminar, has failed at major points.

5. The evidence all points in the direction that the high Christology of the Church has its source in

Jesus and that worship of Jesus as God was there from the beginning.[107]

6. If Jesus was little more than a witty sage or cynic philosopher who spoke only in short pithy sayings or parables, why was he crucified? What threat was he either to the Jewish authorities or the Roman government? Such a Jesus would have challenged certain social and cultural conventions in his day, but this is hardly the kind of activity that gets one nailed to a cross.

7. The work of the Jesus Seminar, in particular, is not really new. It is simply a continuation of the anti-supernatural approach of persons like Rudolf Bultmann who attempted (and failed) to get back to the historical Jesus by means of "demytholization." Strip away anything and everything that looks supernatural and see what is left. The results: such a Jesus could not have inspired worship, much less martyrdom on the part of his followers.

8. The uncertainties of critical scholars and the varied portraits that they paint of Jesus should cause us pause. If they are so fair and objective with the evi-

dence why is it that they cannot even agree among themselves on who Jesus was? Is it perhaps they are guilty of biases, prejudices and agendas that cause them to discover a Jesus very much to their liking? James Edwards with tongue in cheek says, "The Jesus Seminar and Company provides media-grabbing examples of the degree to which contemporary liberal scholarship will go to make Jesus a karaoke crooner of current trends and ideologies."[108]

9. The gospels were written from the standpoint of faith for the purpose of spreading the faith. This is honestly admitted in the biblical texts themselves. This does not lessen their credibility, but actually enhances it.[109]

10. Numerous eyewitnesses were alive when the Gospels were written. They most certainly would have functioned as custodians and protectors of the testimony concerning Jesus.

Though additional evidence could be brought to this study to defend the reliability of the Jesus we find in the Bible, we will end this section with this,

"The most reasonable answer to the question why the Gospels present Jesus as they do is because that is essentially who Jesus was. The Gospels faithfully preserve the memory that he left on his followers, that he was divinely legitimated and empowered to be God's Son and Servant."[110] This is the Jesus of Scripture. This is the Jesus of Church history. This is the Jesus confessed today by the believing Church. This is the Jesus we worship and serve as Lord.

NOTES

[1] John Knox, *The Man Christ Jesus* (Chicago: Willett, Clark and Company, 1941), 54.

[2] Augustine, *Confessions*, as quoted in Jaroslav Pelikan, *Jesus through the Centuries: His Place in the History of Culture* (New Haven: Yale University Press, 1985), 233.

[3] C. S. Lewis, *Mere Christianity* (New York: MacMillan, 1943, 1945, 1952), 54–55.

[4] Ibid., 55–56.

[5] For more on the Old Testament record, see Daniel L. Akin, "The Person of Christ," in *A Theology for the Church*, edited by Daniel L. Akin (Nashville: B&H Academic, 2007), 481-492.

[6] Willem A. VanGemeren, *Psalms*, EBC vol. 5 (Grand Rapids: Zondervan, 1991), 65.

[7] Derek Kidner, *Psalms 1–72*, TDOC (Downers Grove: InterVarsity, 1973), 86.

[8] Kidner, 105.

[9] Grant Osborne, "Crucifixion," *Baker Encyclopedia of the Bible*, vol. 1 ed. by W. A. Elwell (Grand Rapids: Baker, 1988), 555.

[10] In Psalm 110:6 we read, "He will judge the nations, heaping up the dead and crushing the rulers of the whole earth." The word that is translated "rulers" can also mean "heads," which recalls Genesis 3:15, where the LORD had sworn to the serpent that the seed of the woman would crush his "head."

[11] Paul R. House, *Old Testament Theology* (Downers Grove, IL: IVP Academic, 1998), 420.

[12] John Oswalt, *The Book of Isaiah, Chapters 1–39*, NICOT (Grand Rapids: Eerdmans, 1986), 210.

[13] Ibid., 211.

[14] Ibid.

[15] E. J. Young, *The Book of Isaiah, Volume 1, Chapters 1–18* (Grand Rapids: Eerdmans, 1965), 329.

[16] Ibid.

[17] Oswalt, 245.

[18] Young, 335.

[19] Oswalt, 247.

[20] Ibid., 248.

[21] Gleason Archer, *Daniel*, vol. 7, EBC (Grand Rapids: Zondervan, 1985), 90.

[22] Miller, 209.

[23] Walter Kaiser, *Toward Rediscovering the Old Testament* (Grand Rapids: Zondervan, 1987), 109.

[24] *Raleigh News & Observer*, Friday, Feb. 20, 1998, pgs. 1, 10.

[25] For more on these and other New Testament passages, see Daniel L. Akin, "The Person of Christ," 492-508.

[26] F. F. Bruce, *The Gospel of John* (Grand Rapids, MI: William B. Eerdmans Publishing, 1983), 31.

[27] D. A. Carson, *The Gospel According to John* (Grand Rapids: Eerdmans, 1991), 126-28.

[28] The others being Colossians 1:15-20, Ephesians 2:14-16, 1 Timothy 3:16, 1 Peter 3:18, Hebrews 1:13, and perhaps the prologue of John

[29] Peter T. O'Brien, *The Letter to the Ephesians* (Grand Rapids, MI: Wm. B. Eerdmans Publishing Company, 1999), 212-216.

[30] F. F. Bruce, *Philippians* (San Francisco: Harper & Row, 1983), 45.

[31] Ibid, 47.

[32] Ibid., 50-51.

[33] T. L. Trevethan, *Our Joyful Confidence* (Downers Grove: IVP, 1981), 13.

[34] E.K. Simpson and F. F. Bruce, *Commentary on the Epistles to the Ephesians and Colossians,* NICNT (Grand Rapids: Eerdmans, 1957), 192.

[35] F. F. Bruce, *The Epistles to the Colossians, to Philemon, and to the Ephesians* (Grand Rapids, MI: William B. Eerdmans Publishing, 1984, 56-57.

[36] John Calvin, *Commentary on the Epistle to the Colossians,* Calvin's Commentaries, Vol. XXI, translated by William Pringle (Grand Rapids: Baker, 1996, rprt), 149-50.

[37] Kent Hughes, *Colossians and Philemon,* (Westchester: Crossway, 1989), 30.

[38] Curtis Vaughan, *Colossians,* EBC, Vol. 11 (Grand Rapids: Zondervan, 1978), 183.

[39] Vaughan, 185.

[40] Francis Schaeffer, *He Is There And He Is Not Silent* in *The Complete Works Of Francis Schaffer,* Vol. 1 (Wheaton: Crossway, 1982), 276.

[41] Ibid.

[42] Simon Kistemaker, *Hebrews,* NTC (Grand Rapids: Baker,

1984), 29.

[43] Leon Morris, *Hebrews*, BSC (Grand Rapids: Zondervan, 1983), 20.

[44] Peter Bien, "Who Was Jesus," *Life Magazine*, vol. 17 (December, 1994), 66–86.

[45] Ibid.

[46] For more on the virgin birth, see Daniel L. Akin, "The Person of Christ," 508-512.

[47] Robert H. Stein, *Jesus the Messiah* (Grand Rapids, MI: Zondervan, 1996), 65.

[48] Ibid.

[49] Erickson, 752.

[50] Gordon Lewis and Bruce Demarest, *Integrative Theology*, vol. 2 (Grand Rapids: Zondervan, 1990), 274.

[51] Ben Witherington III, "Birth of Jesus," in *Dictionary of Jesus and the Gospels*, ed. Joel B. Green, Scot McKnight and I. Howard Marshall (Downers Grove: InterVarsity, 1992), 72.

[52] Darrell L. Bock, *Luke 1:1–9:50*, BECNT (Grand Rapids: Baker, 1994), 270.

[53] Ibid., 271.

[54] D. A. Carson, *Matthew*, EBC, vol. 8 (Grand Rapids:

Zondervan, 1984), 107.

[55] John Broadus, *Matthew* (Valley Forge: Judson, 1886), 70.

[56] Carson, *Matthew*, 385.

[57] Ibid.

[58] Ibid., 384–85.

[59] The section on the ascension was gleaned from Dr. Jerry Vines, "Our Ascended Lord," Jan. 27, 1976; Paul Enns, *The Moody Handbook of Theology* (Chicago: Moody, 1989), 235; Curtis Vaughn, *Acts* (Grand Rapids: Zondervan, 1974), 15–16; personal class notes for Christian Theology.

[60] John R. W. Stott, *The Cross of Christ* (Downers Grove: IVP, 1986), 7.

[61] For further study on the doctrine of humanity, I would commend Anthony Hoekema, *Created in God's Image* (Grand Rapids: Eerdmans, 1986) and Robert Pyne, *Humanity & Sin* (Nashville: Word, 1999).

[62] Paige Patterson, "Reflections on the Atonement," *CTR* 3 (1989), 312–13.

[63] Ibid., 314.

[64] Stott, 124.

[65] Bettenson, 34-35.

[66] L. Berkhof, *Systematic Theology* (Grand Rapids: Eerd-

mans, 1941), 386–87.

[67] Millard J. Erickson, *Christian Theology* (Nashville: Baker Book House, 1985), 783–85.

[68] Ibid., 788–92.

[69] Berkhof, 389–90.

[70] Stott, 149.

[71] J. I. Packer, "What Did the Cross Achieve? The Logic of Penal Substitution" (Tyndale Biblical Theology Lecture, 1973), 20–21.

[72] Packer, 42–43.

[73] William Lane Craig, *Reasonable Faith: Christian Truth and Apologetics* (Wheaton: Crossway, 1994 rev. ed.), 255.

[74] *Let God Be True* (Brooklyn: Watchtower Bible and Tract Society, rev. ed. 1982), 138.

[75] Ibid., 41. Quoted from Hank Hanegraaff, *Resurrection* (Nashville: Word, 2000), 10.

[76] Quoted in Craig, 269.

[77] Ian Wilson, *Jesus: The Evidence* (San Francisco: Harper & Row, 1984), 141.

[78] Jürgen Moltmann, *The Crucified God*, trans. R. A. Wilson and John Bowden (New York: Harper & Row, 1974), 167-68.

[79] Craig, 279.

[80] Hanegraaff, 7-8. He gives the source of this debate as: William Lane Craig and Robert Greg Cavin, "Dead or Alive? A Debate on the Resurrection of Jesus." (Anaheim, CA: Simon Greenleaf University, 1995), audiotape.

[81] *The Koran*, trans. N. J. Dawood (New York: Penguin, 1956, rev. 1974), 382.

[82] Hanegraaff, 8-9.

[83] Gary Habermas, *The Resurrection of Jesus: A Rational Inquiry* (Ann Arbor, MI: University Microfilms, 1976), especially 114-71.

[84] Gary R. Habermas, "Jesus' Resurrection and Contemporary Criticism: An Apologetic," *Criswell Theological Review* 4, no. 1 (Fall 1989), 167.

[85] Habermas, "Jesus' Resurrection," 163-71.

[86] Ibid., 161-62, emphasis added.

[87] Lee Strobel, *The Case for Christ* (Grand Rapids: Zondervan, 1998), 247.

[88] Craig, 276.

[89] See Craig Blomberg, *The Historical Reliability of the Gospels* (Downers Grove: IVP, 1987); F. F. Bruce, *The New Testament Documents: Are They Reliable?* (Grand Rapids: Eerdmans, 1960).

[90] See also Rom. 6:8-9; 1 Cor. 6:12-14; 2 Cor. 4:14; 5:10; Phil. 3:21; 1 Thess. 4:14; 1 John 3:2.

[91] Gary R. Habermas, "Jesus' Resurrection and Contemporary Criticism: An Apologetic (Part II)" *Criswell Theological Review* 4 (Spring 1990), 384.

[92] Karl Barth, *Dogmatics in Outline*, trans. G. T. Thomson (New York: Philosophical Library, 1949), 114.

[93] Bernard Ramm, *An Evangelical Christology* (Nashville: Nelson, 1985), 9-10.

[94] Daniel L. Akin, *1,2,3 John*, NAC (Nashville: Broadman and Holman, 2001), 29.

[95] *The Apostolic Fathers*, trans. J. B. Lightfoot and J. R. Harmer (Grand Rapids: Baker, 1989), 88.

[96] Ibid., 100.

[97] Cyril Richardson, ed., *Early Church Fathers* (New York: MacMillan, 1970), 378-79.

[98] V. L. Walter, "Ebionites," in *Evangelical Dictionary of Theology 2nd ed.*, ed. Walter Elwell (Grand Rapids: Baker, 2001), 362.

[99] Richardson, 386.

[100] C. C. Kroeger, "Origen" in *Evangelical Dictionary of Theology, 2nd ed.*, ed. Walter Elwell (Grand Rapids: Baker,

2001), 870.

[101] Tertullian, *Against Praxeas* in *The Ante-Nicene Fathers*, vol. III, ed. Rev. Alexander Roberts and James Donaldson (Grand Rapids: Eerdmans, 1997 reprint), 597.

[102] Phillip Schaff, *History of the Christian Church*, vol. 3, *Nicene and Post Nicene Christianity* (Grand Rapids: Eerdmans, 1977), 628.

[103] Epistle 51 of St. Gregory the Theologian to Cledonius, Against Apollinarius.

[104] I wish to express appreciation to Steve Wellum, my former colleague at Southern Seminary for the excellent observations he provides at this point in his notes on Christian Theology.

[105] For more on the quest for the historical Jesus, see Daniel L. Akin, "The Person of Christ," 531-535

[106] Frederick Schleiermacher, *The Christian Faith* (Philadelphia: Fortress, 1976), 97.

[107] Steven Davis, "Why the Historical Jesus Matters," in *Theology News and Notes* (June, 1999).

[108] James Edwards, "Who Do Scholars Say That I Am?" *Christianity Today* (Mar. 4, 1996), 16.

[109] Ibid., 17.

[110] Ibid., 20.

56894260R00104

Made in the USA
Middletown, DE
25 July 2019